ELIZABETH CASTILLO

Dear Healing Heart

Reconnecting with Yourself *While Caring for Your* **Child with Special Needs**

Dear Healing Heart:
Reconnecting With Yourself While Caring for Your Child with Special Needs
Copyright © 2025 by Elizabeth Castillo

979-8-9946736-0-7 (Hardback)
979-8-9946736-1-4 (Paperback)
979-8-9946736-2-1 (eBook)

Library of Congress Cataloging-in-Publication Data

Cover design by Kam Bains

Interior formatting by KUHN Design Group | kuhndesigngroup.com

Printed in the United States of America

To my parents for your unwavering love, support, and resilience.

*To my children and my husband, my heart and
greatest teachers in everything that truly matters.*

*And to every family member, friend, professional, and caring
soul who has walked beside us, thank you for your support,
your kindness, and the light you've woven into our story.*

Contents

It's quiet now. Maybe your child is finally asleep, or you've found a rare moment to breathe. Still, your mind keeps spinning: Am I doing enough? Will tomorrow be easier? Will I handle it better? In the stillness, you wonder if anyone truly sees how much each day requires; how your heart aches in ways others can't fully understand, and how easily your own needs slip to the bottom of the list. I know these questions well. In moments just like this, I found myself searching for answers, and that search has become this letter, from my healing heart to yours.

What follows is my journey along a path that can feel challenging and lonely, yet holds deep love, growth, and an opportunity for healing. It is one of learning to make space for my own heart amid the chaos—and an invitation for you to do the same.

Dear Healing Heart,

I see you. I see how your heart brims with fierce love for your child. I see how it also aches in quiet confusion and tender surrender. I see the exhaustion behind your eyes. The overwhelm tucked into choices for your child's care: therapies, routines, and moments of crisis. I see how you show up with grit and love, even as the dream of how it was supposed to be slowly dissolves into something unexpected. You hold so much: the weight of what is, the memory of what might have been, and the hope for what could still be. And still, I see the joy. I understand the pride you feel in moments others might overlook, but ones that feel monumental to parents like us.

This space? I know it well. The space between holding it all together and quietly falling apart. Between boundless love and relentless fatigue. Between being there for your child and losing pieces of yourself along the way. I'm writing as a fellow parent of a child with special needs. As someone who understands that tender in between. Someone who knows what it means to love deeply while wondering how to keep going and remember that your needs also matter.

We each carry different stories, shaped by our children's unique journeys, our backgrounds, and our distinct temperaments. Yet, there is something universal we share: the invisible weight. The unyielding devotion. The quiet resilience. The deep longing to feel less alone. This journey magnifies the truths of parenting: the sleepless nights, the fierce protectiveness, the aching love. But it also asks something more. It stretches our capacity and adds layers most will never see. We become translators of our child's behavior, advocates in meeting rooms and in our day-to-day life, and bridges between worlds that often feel very far apart.

It's repeatedly explaining your child's needs. It's holding space for their emotions while quietly managing your own. It's finding joy in progress that doesn't match any chart.

It's the midnight research sessions. The waiting rooms where time stretches. The unexpected grief that catches you off guard—at the playground, in casual conversations, or while watching your child struggle with something that comes more easily to others.

It's loving so fiercely that your chest physically aches. It's quietly wondering how long you can carry this intensity.

This path changes you. It teaches you what it means to rise with tenderness. To find grace in chaos. To become someone that you didn't know you needed to be. Yet, underneath it all, that small voice asks, *How do I keep going when the hard moments feel like too much?*

Here's what I've learned: You don't need to have all the answers or get it all right. Your love, your presence, and your efforts all matter more than you know. The invisible work you do, the weight no one else sees, and the pain that lives alongside the deepest love are all real. You deserve to feel seen in all of it. You deserve permission to reconnect with yourself, to reclaim your joy, without an all-consuming guilt for doing so. You deserve to honor your healing process while deeply loving your child.

Introduction

LETTING GO AND REBUILDING

I didn't always believe that letting go was a necessary step in the healing process. For years, I thought strength meant pushing through. I thought love meant self-sacrifice. I gave everything I had until I had nothing left. Eventually, I didn't just feel tired; I felt lost. Disconnected from peace. From joy. From myself. My nervous system lived in overdrive, and I didn't know how to stop. I drowned out my own voice beneath the noise and the doing.

In time, I burned out. All of it consumed me until I reached a breaking point. I finally began to listen to the voice I'd been drowning out. The voice that was reminding me, *You don't have to live like this. There's another way. A softer, steadier, more whole way.* I had to make hard choices. Some meant letting go of dreams I'd held tightly. Others meant releasing patterns that no longer served my family or me. I would have to let go of the version of me I thought I had to be. I was being called to face the grief and the love, the joy and the fear, and to dismantle the life I had always known, and slowly, courageously rebuild from the inside out.

I would also need to learn how to be present, how to ask for help, how to honor my own needs without feeling guilty for doing so, and how to find joy in the small moments instead of expecting monumental ones. This wasn't a one-time shift; it became a practice. Some days, choosing softness over strength took everything I had. Other days, I simply chose to rest instead of push. But it was in that softness that I began to reconnect with my child, with myself, and with the life that had always been waiting underneath the weight I'd been carrying. Perhaps my truth and some of the practices that carried me through will also offer you a gentler way forward.

WHY I'M SHARING MY STORY

Parenting a child with special needs changes you. It asks for a different kind of strength. One woven from advocacy and surrender, resilience and softness. There are endless resources for our children, such as therapies, interventions, and specialists, and yes, those are essential, but what about us? The ones doing the holding? For years, I longed for a place where I could be real. A space where I could openly say, "I'm overwhelmed. I'm struggling. I'm doing my best, and often, it still doesn't feel like enough!" A space without judgment. Without fixing. A space where I had the right to feel it all. I needed a space where my voice could express it all: the fierce love, the joy, the heartbreak, and the heaviness. I needed permission to say, "This is beautiful *and* hard!" Both things can be true. This book was born from that ache, that space I so desperately needed.

WHAT YOU'LL FIND IN THESE PAGES

This book follows the path of my own journey from pain and struggle to gradually remembering that I also matter in this story, and to a place of integration and becoming, a process that is always evolving. Each chapter begins with a personal story, and then I share insights and professional guidance that have carried me through. At the end of each chapter is a Reader Reflection with gentle prompts for journaling or quiet contemplation, as well as some simple practices that may resonate. I close with an affirmation, a grounding reminder for the moments when you need it most. This book isn't about doing more. It's about coming home to yourself in the midst of it all.

THE TRUTH ABOUT THIS JOURNEY

I still have hard days. On many mornings, I've already felt a day's worth of emotions before nine a.m. There were many times while writing this book that I had to step away, overwhelmed by my own heavy days and seasons. I thought, *Who am I to offer support or hope when I don't have any to give right now?* But that's the journey: learning to come back and to be gentle with ourselves when we need to step away and come back when we're ready to try again.

Healing began when I stopped running from my feelings and started offering myself the same compassion I so freely gave to others. Sometimes, that means asking my child for forgiveness when I've been short-tempered or overwhelmed. Sometimes, it means forgiving myself for the moments I couldn't hold it all with grace. And often, it just means pausing, breathing, and reminding myself: *This is enough. Right here. Right now.* Special needs parenting is sacred and messy and miraculous. It asks everything of you, and then asks again. That's why it's okay to rest. It's okay to not know what's next.

It's okay to ask for more support. Some seasons feel light, and others feel very heavy—both are part of the journey.

BEFORE WE BEGIN

These pages do not offer a grand solution or a magic formula to make everything okay. Instead, they offer a companion. Someone to walk alongside you through the struggles and the victories that others might not fully understand. This path can feel confusing and exhausting. It can also bring unexpected joy and profound connection. All these feelings are valid, and they don't mean you are failing; they simply mean that you are human, walking a path that asks a lot of you. There is no right pace here, only your own timing. Take what feels right and leave behind what doesn't. Remember that you and your child are enough. Your love matters. Most importantly, your heart and your story matter. Take a breath, and let's begin together.

The Thing

THE MOMENT EVERYTHING CHANGES

It happens in an instant. A phone call. A meeting. A quiet phrase spoken by a professional, carefully worded yet impossible to unhear. You're handed something that doesn't quite feel like news. It feels like a gentle shifting of the ground beneath you. It's something invisible yet irreversible: A diagnosis. In the days that follow, everything starts to feel different. The schedule you once knew no longer makes sense. The vision of parenthood you carried begins to unravel, not because your love has changed, but because the path ahead suddenly looks nothing like you imagined. And though you don't know it yet, in time, you will also be different.

WHEN THE SIGNS BEGIN TO WHISPER

For some, the news of a diagnosis comes before their child is even born, through screenings, blood tests, or a quiet observation from a doctor. You're handed news before ever meeting your baby. For others, it arrives within the first fragile days after birth, when complications arise or differences become visible. For others, like me, it emerges slowly. A light whisper that gradually takes shape and insists on being heard.

The path leading up to *my* moment unfolded gradually, a slow accumulation of tiny signs that didn't seem like much on their own, but over time, they revealed a clearer picture. Those early months felt "typical" enough: sleepless nights, baby milestones, and that familiar cocktail of new mom bliss and exhaustion. My daughter was pure joy: smiley, social, curious. The red flags people often mention simply weren't there. In hindsight, there were differences, but I was a new mom surviving on instinct, not searching for things I didn't yet know to look for.

Around seven months, subtle shifts began to surface. Delayed milestones. Movements that seemed slightly off. She would engage and smile during play, but wouldn't imitate simple gestures like clapping or waving—milestones considered typical by most checklists. She could sit up, but her core strength and stability were weak. Gentle observations from my mom and others helped me see through the fog and encouraged me to start asking questions. That's when the search began. One specialist led to another. Appointments, evaluations, and endless intake forms—each step brought hope that someone might finally make sense of what we were seeing. Eventually, we were given a diagnosis, though it was unclear and vague. No clear roadmap; just question marks where answers were supposed to be.

My *moment* came to life on an ordinary Tuesday morning in a sterile exam room as I sat cradling my daughter with my mom and husband beside us. The doctor came in, greeted us, and began to share words I couldn't fully take in. Medical terms. Test results. Explanations that started to blur together. I watched her mouth move, her expressions shifting as she spoke, but soon, the words drifted further away. I stopped listening. The room grew quiet, and suddenly, I went numb. I couldn't react or even form the questions I should have asked. Instead, I pulled on my armor. I nodded as if I understood, acting as though nothing life-altering had just been said. I held my daughter close and pretended the ground beneath us hadn't just shifted. And just like that, what I would later call *"The Thing"* was born.

HOW *THE THING* COMES TO LIFE

The Thing is what happens when words on a page begin to shape your life. At first, the diagnosis (or *The Thing*) felt distant, something clinical that didn't seem quite real. My daughter did have a diagnosis, but it didn't come with a common name or an easy way to describe it to people, so calling it *The Thing* felt simpler, softer, and easier to share. And for some families, there isn't a diagnosis at all. Just a *Thing* that is very real in your life, without a clear label or explanation as to why.

Looking back, I didn't cry. I didn't fall apart. I didn't even react. I pushed *The Thing* and my own emotions aside and prepared for war. But over time, *The Thing* grew. It began to influence everything. It found its way into every conversation, every form, every plan. It altered how I saw my child and how I saw myself. It made me question my worth and my child's worth.

The Thing is not the diagnosis alone. It's the space it takes up in your life and the feelings that come with it. It's in the way it shows up when you're filling out forms (for school, medical care, or services), and there's a section asking about "extra concerns." It's there when other parents casually mention their child's latest achievement, and you calculate silently whether your child has reached that milestone yet. It's present in the way you phrase things: "She's doing really well … considering." It hovers when you watch other families engage in outings and activities more easily, wondering if they notice the differences, too. Ultimately, *The Thing* isn't about a label in a medical file. It's what it means for you as a parent, quietly navigating a path you never expected to walk.

The Thing is the paperwork, the missed playdates because therapy appointments come first, the new language of goals, services, and supports, the silent weight in the room when you hear another parent brag about milestones. You didn't mean for it to take over, but little by little, it did. And often, *The Thing* becomes *Things*—additional discoveries, new evaluations, and emerging differences as time goes on. Each new layer shifts the ground again, asking you to widen your understanding and your heart.

THE LIFE YOU BUILT, NOW TRANSFORMED

Before, your world made sense. There were benchmarks. Schedules. Advice that applied. You had internalized expectations: first words arriving on time, easy playdates where you could chat with other parents while the kids played independently, the rhythm of school activities and celebrations. You expected parenthood to be guided by instinct, by tradition, by what you had learned through your own upbringing. You braced for the usual worries: skinned knees, homework battles, and choosing between soccer and piano lessons.

These weren't just hopes; they were the invisible framework that shaped your understanding of what life would look like. And now, that framework is dissolving. Suddenly, the rules have been rewritten. Birthday parties are no longer fun get-togethers, but sensory experiences to be planned with care. Will there be loud music? Crowds?

Unexpected schedule changes? Preschool means both circle time *and* therapy sessions. Outings come with backup plans and exit strategies.

You're learning a whole new language, one that wasn't in the parenting books. Instead of googling *when do toddlers start talking*, you're researching speech therapy techniques and AAC devices. Instead of comparing preschool curricula, you're asking about IEP support and sensory breaks. Your Google search history becomes a bleak reminder of your new reality: *sensory integration activities, how to explain disability to siblings, developmental pediatrician near me.*

The hardest part? In all this newness, it's easy to forget your child's core identity. Instead, you might see them as their diagnosis, bravely navigating the world. But they're still the beautiful, whole, wondrous being you've always loved. The one who lights up at music. The one with that infectious giggle. The one who finds joy in the simplest things that others pay little attention to. And you (beneath the advocacy, the appointments, and the careful coordination) haven't lost yourself either.

THE INITIATION

What no one told me (and what I wasn't prepared for) is that I hadn't just received a diagnosis for my child; I had been initiated into something much bigger than I understood. It wasn't as simple as learning to parent differently. I was being called to change the way I would operate as a parent at my core. I would have to revisit long-held beliefs about control and how life "should" unfold. I would also be reevaluating the assumptions about what makes a good parent and the stories I'd told myself about my child and my future.

This shift wasn't about tweaking a few things. I would have to start over with a new foundation—from planning everything anew to adapting as we went, from worrying about the future to focusing on the present moment, and from comparing to celebrating what was ours. I had to figure out which parts of me would help and which ones needed to change. My easygoing temperament and practical skills have served me well in many situations, especially where I had to be flexible and roll with surprises and unexpected changes, but I found myself battling my overly critical mind, especially toward myself. I had always held myself to impossibly high standards. Later, I would have to confront an overwhelming emotional landscape that I had ignored for far too long, making everything feel even heavier than it already was.

I also had to develop new strengths, becoming more organized than I'd ever been, keeping track of endless appointments, managing therapies, and the bills that came with both. I also had to let go of things that weren't working anymore: old ideas about what success for my child looked like and the developmental timeline I'd imagined. I would learn to stop measuring both my child and myself against others, to celebrate the victory of connection and communication in whatever form it took, and to reevaluate the nature of independence and how that process would evolve over the years, celebrating every triumph, no matter how long each task took or what the result looked like.

WHAT COMES NEXT

My initiation had already begun. My transformation was already underway, even if I wasn't seeing it yet. The path ahead will stretch and soften you. It will break open parts of you that were never meant to stay closed. Some days will bring grief and grace in the same breath. You'll discover strengths you didn't know you had. Ultimately, you'll realize you weren't broken; you were being remade. *The Thing* is not your child's whole story, and it's not your whole story either. The journey from that first overwhelming moment of diagnosis eventually transitions into something softer, steadier, more whole—the questions you never thought to ask and the unexpected answers that slowly emerge, and the experience and the wisdom you gain along the way, eventually allowing you to give *The Thing* its proper place. No more, no less. But before any of that can happen, it's time to work. The "doing phase" arrives as you pour yourself into research, therapies, and appointments for your child. It's about building a new rhythm around this new reality.

READER REFLECTION:
Naming the Thing

Take a moment to sit with these questions. There are no right or wrong answers, only your truth. Remember: *The Thing* is just a thing. Your story is still being written.

- What is *The Thing* in your story?

- What do you remember about the moment you received confirmation of *The Thing* (a diagnosis or developmental difference)? What did that moment feel like?

- How has *The Thing* shaped your daily life? When does it feel most overwhelming?

- What expectations about parenthood have shifted for you? How does your reality compare to what you once imagined?

- How much power does *The Thing* currently hold in your child's and your story? What would it look and feel like to give it its rightful place, no more, no less?

AFFIRMATION

This is the start of a journey I am being called to walk. The thing does not define my worth or my child's worth. I trust that I have what it takes.

CHAPTER 2

The Doing

WHEN ACTION BECOMES ARMOR

When faced with *The Thing* and all the unknown that comes with it, most of us direct our efforts into action. We naturally focus on what we can do for our child instead of sitting with our feelings, believing that if we do enough, we can somehow stay ahead of the emotional storm. Maybe that's all we can do because the full weight of what we're facing is too much to absorb all at once. The phase that comes after the arrival of *The Thing* looks different for everyone, even though it usually includes the onset of therapies, medical appointments, and sometimes, increasing medical emergencies. But underneath it all, we carry the same relentless drive: a need to do something, *anything*, in response to the reality that is unfolding.

BUILDING FROM SCRATCH

For me, the drive began with throwing myself into researching therapy options. I wasn't one to obsessively research my daughter's diagnosis and what it did or didn't mean, but rather to research my plan of action and immediately put it into play. We landed at a therapy center that was part of the main children's hospital in our area, with multiple locations throughout the city. I called and was given an appointment. Not right away because availability was limited, but it was a starting point.

When we walked in for her appointment, a wave of overwhelm immediately washed over me. It was a large place with a children's urgent care neighboring it. The waiting room was crowded and the paperwork extensive. They took us in for an evaluation. The therapists were very kind, so that wasn't the issue—it was the long list of questions that felt brutal, the way my daughter cried when they performed certain routine observations that were uncomfortable for her, and the way I sat there watching, processing what was happening, feeling unsure of what lay ahead. After completing the evaluation, they told us we would hear from the office soon. A few days turned into a little over a week, and then we had to wait even longer because appointments were hard to come by.

This is where the doing starts to feel heavy, and why we propel ourselves into research and are called to forge a path. The options usually come with obstacles, especially through larger programs. Subsequently, we were sent to an early intervention government program. We were advised to do this to essentially get her in "the system," which was easier at a young age versus when the child is older. They did an evaluation and offered two short sessions a week, which was far from what my daughter needed. Again, I encountered disappointment, questions, and not enough care, all of which are a large part of this journey. Then came the harsh realization: I would have to do much of this work on my own.

I started asking around and researching smaller centers that would be easier to visit multiple times a week with more personalized access to therapists. In my daughter's case, her diagnosis wasn't common and didn't check the boxes neatly, but her plan of care included as much therapy and care as possible, especially since she was young and in a crucial developmental window. We eventually landed at a smaller private center where she would begin occupational and physical therapy, then, eventually, speech therapy numerous times a week. I wasn't just managing a plan; I was piecing together a puzzle with no clear guidelines. The calendar became a constant juggle of appointments and gaps I tried to fill. I learned a new language: muscle tone, sensory processing, and developmental windows. Each new professional brought more observations, more suggestions, and more thoughts to bombard my already overloaded mind. And even though the calendar was full, it never felt like enough.

THE DRIVING BELIEF

At some point, the doing stopped focusing solely on her development. It became about trying to change our reality. In a way, I started to believe that if I worked hard enough, if I found the right combination of therapies and specialists, then we might be able to outrun *The Thing* altogether. I didn't realize this right away. It actually took years of frantic work before I saw what my drive was actually about.

In that moment, it felt like maybe if I did enough, the gap between where she was and where she "should" be would close. Maybe I could change our story. Maybe the diagnosis would become irrelevant. Hope looked like action: the endless research sessions, the specialist with a long waitlist, and the program that promised rapid progress. Every step forward felt like proof that more doing would yield bigger results. What I didn't realize then was that the doing had become its own kind of coping, a way to feel in control while avoiding the grief and fear I wasn't ready to face.

THE ENDLESS SEARCH

We began with traditional therapies, but over time, she tried everything. I enrolled her in various intensive programs that were named after foreign specialists offering hope and promise. I drove for an hour each way every Saturday morning for her to attend a twenty-five-minute equine therapy session. If there was even a sliver of hope, we chased it. Each therapy felt like a possibility. Each scheduled appointment felt like progress.

I wore my overpacked calendar like a badge of honor, proof that I was doing everything I could. The busier I was, the more it felt like I was moving us forward. But deep down, it always felt like there was more to do, more to fix. Another therapy. Another specialist. Another approach that might finally be the answer. While other families were at mommy-and-me groups, we were at therapies and appointments.

I hadn't given myself space to feel. I never paused to grieve or even to breathe. I was trying to stay ahead of the emotional reckoning I didn't want to face. I was so focused on the next milestone that I missed some quieter moments of connection. Of course, I enjoyed plenty of quality time with my daughter, but I was also buried under the weight of getting it right. I wanted to fix, to optimize, to problem-solve. Most interactions with my daughter were filtered through the lens of development and progress. And in time, I started to unravel.

THE UNRAVELING

My behavior toward my daughter and her progress became reactive instead of being fueled by motivation. The excitement I once had for new therapies faded. The research that once energized me became exhausting. I kept showing up, but the exhaustion (physical and emotional) was impossible to ignore. A growing numbness crept in. I felt disconnected from myself and went through the motions of each day without feeling fully present. I was trying to balance it all (work, life, "fixing"), but each time, I was being pulled further away from myself. I eventually disappeared into the role of manager and advocate, unsure if this was just how it was supposed to be.

Beneath the surface, the pressure was mounting. It soon became a quiet resentment, a fear that I wasn't doing enough, or maybe I was doing too much. Even as I became more skilled at navigating the system, I grew more depleted. Burnout was creeping in. I was slipping into depression. The constant doing was straining my closest relationships. And still, I kept pushing—until I couldn't push anymore.

THE BREAKING POINT

My breaking point didn't arrive in a single dramatic moment. It took years of living at this overwhelming pace before things eventually caught up with me. By then, it was no longer a whisper. It was a force shouting at me, and it was everywhere: staring out the window in traffic while driving home from yet another therapy session and feeling too drained to search for the next option presented to us. As she grew older and her needs changed, it hung over my head as I navigated endless cycles of research for schools and programs, each one less suited to her needs and demanding more advocacy and accommodations.

Family and friends started making remarks out of concern and love. At some point, I had to stop defending myself and acknowledge what they were seeing: I was disappearing into the endless pursuit of the next solution. What once felt like progress began to feel like pressure. The calendar I once clung to now felt like a trap. A breakfast date with my dad became a crucial turning point. As we ate, we naturally started talking about my daughter's progress and current schedule. After some time, his expression changed, and he calmly asked, "How are you doing in all of this?"

I had to pause and think. In that pause, I realized I didn't stop to consider myself that often. I couldn't come up with an answer. I didn't know how I was doing, but I did know I was tired, overwhelmed, and battling a sadness I couldn't shake. I had essentially lost myself in the doing. And then came the next question: "How do you plan to continue like this?" His questions hit me hard. The realization came crashing down like a ton of bricks. *How was I going to sustain this pace? More importantly, what was my intention with all of this?* This simple breakfast conversation shook me. I wondered, *How do I factor myself into this story again? Why don't I think I deserve to feel differently despite the challenges I'm being called to face?*

I replayed the conversation repeatedly, and then I started asking myself, *Where am I going? What am I trying to do? And at what cost?* After spending time with these questions, feeling confused and defeated by my overwhelm, I realized something had to give. I needed to reclaim myself in all of this. My needs and my emotions also mattered in this story. Loving myself enough to prioritize my mental health would benefit everyone around me. But to reclaim myself, I first had to understand how I'd gotten here. I had lost sight of the intention behind all the doing. The life I had built, fueled by constant action, was no longer sustainable. And then an even harder realization hit me: The gap I had been trying so hard to close wasn't my daughter's; it was actually mine.

WHAT WAS IT REALLY ABOUT?

I had been so focused on building my daughter's skills that I had neglected to build my own capacity to be with my emotions. You can't research your way past fear. You can't schedule your way out of emotional reckoning. The therapies weren't the problem; they were essential. They still are. Advocacy was necessary in a system that doesn't offer enough. But somewhere along the way, the doing became the only thing I allowed myself to feel competent at. It crowded out space for the very emotions that needed tending.

I had been chasing an impossible standard of enough: enough therapy, enough progress, enough improvement to somehow make the diagnosis irrelevant. But "enough" wasn't a number or a milestone. Over time, I would learn to trust our new version of enough. I would realize that *The Thing* didn't have to be the enemy, but rather something to integrate and gently place within our story. But to understand this, I had to be willing to stop running and start facing what I had been avoiding for so long: my emotional landscape. It wasn't comfortable, but it was necessary.

READER REFLECTION:
Your Way Forward

- If you've experienced burnout before, what resonates with you in my story? What would you tell your earlier self now that you've lived through it?

- If you're early on in the journey, what lessons can you take from my story? How might you protect yourself from taking on too much pressure or responsibility?

- What does your child's current schedule look like? Make a list of therapies, appointments, and routines that fill your week. Do you feel like you're doing too much, too little, or the right amount? Equally important, how do you feel within your current rhythm?

- What's driving your "doing"? Is it clarity and conscious choice, or fear and outside pressure? Are you caught in the trap of over-researching, over-planning, or trying to control too many variables at once?

- What needs to shift? Is there anything you can gently remove, delegate, or simplify? What small, realistic changes could help you feel more aligned with what truly matters?

AFFIRMATION

*I can take meaningful action
without losing myself in the process.*

CHAPTER 3

The Emotional Landscape

THE HEART OF THE JOURNEY

Special needs parenting doesn't just change your daily routine; it reshapes your entire emotional world. It begins when *The Thing* starts to reveal itself, and the emotions that come as a result can feel vast and consuming, especially early on. When it comes to our emotions and how they relate to our child, it's rarely just one feeling at a time. It's usually layers upon layers, often contradictory and always shifting. Confusion, sadness, and disbelief can hit you all at once, each one colliding with the next. In the next moment, love, pride, and joy hit you just as hard. Grief and joy can happen in the same breath. Fear and awe are often intertwined. Love and exhaustion dance side by side. These emotions don't follow a predictable path; they circle back, collide, evolve, and catch you off guard with their depth and persistence. Every emotion you carry (hope and fear, pride and guilt, anger and love) deserves space. These emotions are not to be fixed or solved. They are to be seen, felt, and honored as part of your humanity. You are not alone in any of it.

THE HIDDEN STRUGGLE

The inner world of parents who have a child with unique needs is frequently overlooked, not just by others but by ourselves. Society praises us for being strong, resourceful, and devoted. We're called "super parents" and told we're "inspiring." But few people ask how we're really doing emotionally. Even fewer create space for us to fall apart when we need to. For years, I dutifully carried it all. I kept moving, kept managing, and kept showing up for every appointment, every advocacy battle, and every sleepless night. But I ignored the emotional weight that accompanied each one. My body became a container for feelings that I was not ready to process. Exhaustion settled into my bones. Brain fog became my baseline. Simple tasks felt heavy. In time, I felt disconnected from myself, from my body's signals, and from the emotions I'd been pushing down for so long.

And here's what many don't tell you: It's often later in this journey, after the initial scrambling and surviving, after you've learned the terminology and navigated the systems, that the weight of it all finally lands. You might find yourself in an unexpectedly quiet moment, suddenly face to face with everything you've been too busy to fully process. The adrenaline slows, life forces a pause, and there you are, confronting what you hadn't fully dealt with before: your own heart.

FINDING MY WAY THROUGH

For too long, I kept pushing through, pretending I was fine. Eventually, my body couldn't keep up. Everything I had been holding in collapsed. Fatigue, depression, and disconnection spilled into every part of my life. When my heart and body could no longer hold it all, I finally understood that something had to change. I needed to slow down and reach out for help. For me, that meant making space for stillness, finding support through therapy, and eventually, seeking medical guidance to help me carry what had become too heavy on my own. I needed to breathe again, to remind my body that I was safe, that it was okay to rest, and that survival didn't have to be the only way to live.

In therapy, I found a sanctuary where I could completely unravel without judgment. I began exploring my emotional landscape in ways I'd never done before. In those quiet moments, I allowed my nervous system to rest and let thoughts and emotions come and go with ease. At first, I naturally resisted some of these emotions. In time, I grew more comfortable and vulnerable to where I could observe them gently without needing to immediately fix or change anything. Through breakdowns and brutally honest conversations, I slowly began reconnecting with myself and naming the emotions I'd spent years burying beneath relentless action.

One of the most transformative shifts in this journey came when I learned to name what I was feeling. Once I could name my emotions, I began to understand them. And when I could understand them, I could finally work with them instead of against them. My therapist also suggested I speak to my primary care doctor to see if there were ways she could help with my emotional state, which felt very heavy and consuming at the time. At one appointment, where I explained how I was feeling, she suggested medication as an emotional support tool. Or, as she put it, "something to provide some relief."

At first, I was overwhelmed by the suggestion and found my mind racing with thoughts. *Does medication mean I can't handle my healing process? Is there something wrong with me? Am I having a bigger reaction to my daughter's issues than I should? Am I weak for needing this? What will people think? Am I giving up? Will I have to take this forever?* As she saw the look on my face and noticed my mind was probably spiraling, she calmly looked at me and asked a simple question: "How are you feeling emotionally right now?" My answer was instant and simple: "Overwhelmed and not good." That was the only answer I needed from myself in that moment.

Many people struggle with the decision to take medication, or it simply may not be for them, and that's perfectly okay, but in my case, it was more about the stories in my mind than having a problem with what the doctor was recommending. That moment of honesty cut through all the overthinking and helped me realize I didn't need to beat myself up about something that could help me. It came down to recognizing that my emotional state was struggling, like any other symptom that deserves attention and care.

The reality was that medication became another tool in my growing list of resources, such as therapy and the quiet moments I was learning to create. Medication didn't signal defeat, nor was it magic, but it became a small bridge that created space for me to do my real work, lifting a little of the heavy emotional cloud that had been hanging overhead. Through this therapeutic work and support, I began to understand the deeper patterns beneath my emotions. For the first time, I understood that my emotional pain deserved the same tenderness and care as any physical wound.

And this journey wasn't just about my daughter. I discovered that so much of what I was struggling with was actually about me, not her. While I thought the emotional burden was about managing her needs and situation, I came to understand that most of my struggle was my own internal work (my patterns, responses, and unprocessed emotions) that needed attention. That exploration became the start of something powerful for me and, as a result, my family. In time, I realized my feelings weren't flaws to be corrected; they were and continue to be signals guiding me toward what I need: rest, support, boundaries, and sometimes, professional help to process things more clearly.

If you're struggling with whether to seek help via therapy, medical guidance, or both, know that getting support shows you are prioritizing self-care. Sometimes, we need different kinds of help at different times. The insights I'm sharing come not from professional training but from walking this path and doing the difficult and vulnerable work of exploring my own emotional landscape. Sometimes, seeing these emotions written down can help you recognize what you've been carrying, offering a breath of relief or a quiet moment of "me too." The more we allow ourselves to acknowledge our emotions (not to fix them, but to examine them), and the more we give ourselves permission to seek whatever support we need, we can begin to find peace with being human in all its complexity.

THE FOUNDATION: GRIEF AND LOVE

Of all the emotions that surface on this journey, grief and love coexisting may be the hardest to wrap your head around, and the most important to talk about. The grief I'm talking about isn't the kind people discuss openly. Some may wonder, *But my child is here with me. Isn't grief about the absence of a person?* I get it, it feels strange to even say it out loud, and part of me used to worry that it would sound ungrateful, but it's not about that at all.

The grief special-needs parents face is about letting go of how we expected parenthood, or life, to look. It's that gentle ache that rises when you realize things turned out differently than the picture you once held in your mind. The milestones you imagined, the routines you dreamed of, and the path you thought you'd walk have all shifted. It doesn't mean you love your child any less; it just means your heart is making room for a new story.

This grief catches you off guard. It can come from watching other kids play and do things that don't come as easily to your child, or from realizing that they may never be able to do those things. It can happen when you receive an invitation to a party or event that makes your stomach flip as you think of the extra work that goes into these outings, even though you are also grateful for the invite. It can show up in conversations with other parents that highlight just how different your world has become. What's complicated is how this grief lives right next to the deepest love you've ever felt. You can miss the future you pictured while being completely in love with the child in front of you. It's not a contradiction; it's just what loving someone with your whole heart looks like. Love brought you here. It's what keeps you going through sleepless nights, those exhausting meetings, and all the moments when you refuse to give up. This love is fierce. It stays up researching, fights for what your child needs, and celebrates the tiniest victories that no one else notices.

Here's what I've learned: Grief is love that doesn't know where to go. You wouldn't feel the loss so deeply if you didn't love so completely. These two feelings fuel everything else. Neither grief nor love runs on a schedule. They show up whenever they want—during meetings, at family dinners, and in those quiet moments when you're watching your child sleep. And honestly? That's okay. Having these feelings doesn't mean you don't adore your child; it means you're human, a parent with a heart big enough to hold the dream, the reality, the loss, and the gift, all at once.

THE EMOTIONS THAT DANCE TOGETHER

While grief and love form the foundation of this journey, they only scratch the surface of so many emotions that come up as we navigate the depths of our emotional world. The other emotions that follow range from light to heavy and can come and go in a breath, reappearing during different seasons or when new challenges or victories arise.

Fear: Living with the Unknown

Fear often lingers beneath the surface, showing up in countless forms. *What if I'm not doing enough? What if my child struggles forever? What if I can't hold it all together? What will happen as my child gets older? How will I support my child and afford all the extra care that they will need? What if something happens to me? Who will care for my child with the same devotion?* The fear can be paralyzing. It whispers that you're failing, that you should be doing more, trying harder, researching deeper. It keeps you awake at night, cycling through scenarios and contingency plans. It makes you question every decision, every therapy choice, every moment of rest you dare to take. Fear isn't failure. It's love with nowhere to land yet. You can acknowledge the fear and still choose courage.

Guilt: The Constant Companion

Guilt looks like losing our temper. When you need a break. When you feel joy, even though your child is struggling. When you feel angry, reactive, or resentful. When you compare your child to others, even silently. When you wonder if you caused their diagnosis somehow, or if you're doing enough to help. Guilt shows up as the voice that says you should be more patient, more understanding, more grateful. It questions your every need for rest, your moments of frustration, and your human limitations. It makes you feel selfish for wanting things to be easier or different. Guilt often feels like caring, but it's usually fear turned inward.

Anger: The Fire Beneath

Anger can show up as tears, irritability, or a slow burn that builds over time. You might feel angry at your spouse or family, at systems that are broken, at friends or strangers who don't understand, at professionals who dismiss your concerns, or at a world that wasn't built with your child's needs in mind. Sometimes, you're angry at yourself; angry for not being more patient, for not advocating harder, for the thoughts you have that you wish you didn't. Sometimes, you're angry at your child, then you feel guilty for that anger, creating a cycle that's hard to break. Anger often comes from grief and feeling powerless. It tells you what matters deeply to you.

Sadness: Witnessing the Struggle

Sadness is different from grief. It isn't about what was imagined; it's about what you live and witness every day: when other children stare or dismiss your child, when the world doesn't understand your child or what they may need, or when you sit through another evaluation, holding back tears. Sadness shows up when you watch your child try so hard for something that seems effortless for their peers. It's there when you see them excluded, when systems fail them, when progress feels impossibly slow. It's the weight of witnessing their struggles while being unable to carry the burden for them. This sadness is love in its most tender form. It hurts because you care so deeply.

Shame: The Quiet Weight We Hide

Shame whispers, "You should be doing more. You shouldn't feel this way. You're not like the other parents. Other parents are handling this better than you. You're broken. You're not enough. Your child is not enough." Shame is different from guilt. Guilt says, "I did something wrong." Shame says, "I am wrong." It shows up when you compare yourself to others and feel like you don't measure up. It makes you hide your struggles and pretend everything is fine. It makes you feel isolated. When we name shame and talk about it, it starts to lose its power over us.

Resentment: The Unspoken Weight

You might feel resentment toward your spouse when they don't understand your emotional process, or when your parenting styles clash. Toward family and friends who offer advice, often too much of it, but then disappear when hands-on help is needed. When friends or family stop including you because accommodating your child feels complicated. You might even feel it when everything seems to fall on your shoulders while other parents move through life with the freedom and ease you no longer have. Sometimes, that resentment flares toward strangers, too. Those who are unkind or so far removed from your family's reality that they can't begin to understand or empathize. Resentment isn't personal toward your child. It's about the unfairness of the situation, the isolation, and the burnout. It's about carrying more than what feels sustainable while watching others who seem to carry so much less. Resentment is usually about unmet needs—your need for support, for understanding, for things to be fair.

Loneliness: Isolated Even in Crowds

You can be surrounded by people and still feel alone. This is not because you aren't loved, but because your experience feels unseen. You long to be understood, to have someone who truly gets what you're going through without explanation. The loneliness shows up in conversations where you can't relate, in moments when you need support but don't know how to ask for it, and in the silence of carrying burdens that feel too heavy to share. This loneliness shows us how much we need understanding and connection with others who get it or simpy see us.

Disappointment: When Reality Falls Short

Disappointment shows up when reality doesn't match your expectations, when the therapy doesn't work as hoped, when the medication causes side effects, when the school system fails your child, and when progress is slower than you'd hoped or stalls altogether. Disappointment happens when what we hoped for doesn't match what's happening. That gap can be very difficult. Sometimes, it's not even one big moment—it's the small letdowns that slowly wear you down. It's the quiet ache of realizing that even your best efforts can't always shift the outcome.

THE SHIFT: WHEN LIGHT SHOWS UP

As you learn to hold both grief and love with compassion, space opens for other emotions. You find yourself recognizing hope, wonder, and moments of unexpected joy that were always there.

Hope: The Light That Keeps You Going

Hope shows up in unexpected places. It's there when you see a flicker of progress, when a new therapy shows promise, and when your child surprises you with a breakthrough you didn't see coming. It's the feeling that whispers, "Tomorrow might be different. Maybe easier or better for both." Hope isn't naive optimism. It's the quiet strength that keeps you going even on the hardest days. It's what gets you up for the next appointment, the next try, the next possibility. Hope lives in the space between what is and what could be. It doesn't deny the challenges; it believes in possibilities beyond them.

Gratitude: The Genuine Kind

This isn't the forced gratitude that others expect you to feel. It's not the "at least" and "you should be thankful" kind. This is the genuine gratitude that rises naturally in quiet moments. Gratitude for the professionals who truly see your child, for the small victories that mean everything, for your child's laugh that hasn't changed despite everything else that has, for the other parents who understand without explanation, and for your own resilience that surprises you. This gratitude doesn't erase the hard parts; it coexists with them. You can be grateful for your child's unique perspective while still grieving the challenges they face.

Wonder: Seeing Through Their Eyes

Your child will show you things you never would have noticed otherwise: the way they find joy in the smallest details, their different way of experiencing the world that becomes a gift to you, and the beauty they see that others walk past. Wonder arrives when you stop trying to force your child into boxes they were never meant to fill and start seeing the world through their eyes, and when their personality shines so bright it outweighs everything else. Wonder reminds you that different doesn't mean less; it means seeing beauty in new ways.

Pride: The Quiet Victories

Pride shows up in the little things. A first word or new words emerging. A breakthrough. An IEP meeting that finally feels like a win. Your child's determination. Your own resilience. Those small moments of progress that others might not even notice but mean the world to you. It's the warmth that rises in your chest when you pause long enough to see what's unfolding. These victories—no matter how small—deserve to be celebrated. Pride doesn't make the hard days disappear; it simply reminds you that you're moving forward, one step at a time.

Joy: The Light That Finds You

Joy often shows up quietly. In funny faces, shared looks, or laughter you didn't see coming. It's your child's personality shining through, their unique way of seeing the world, and the moments when *The Thing* takes a backseat, and you can smile again. Joy doesn't mean everything is okay; it means you're still here. Still feeling. Still open to the light that finds its way through the cracks.

Relief: When the Weight Lifts

Relief comes and goes, just like the harder emotions. It's there when a difficult phase passes, when you find the right support, when you realize you're stronger than you thought. Relief isn't permanent, but it's real. Let yourself feel it fully when it comes. These moments of lightness are not luxuries; they're necessities that restore your spirit for what comes next.

Connection: The Unexpected Bonds

Some of the deepest connections form through shared struggle: the bond with your child that grows stronger through navigating challenges together, the kinship with other special needs parents who understand without explanation, the professionals who become allies in your child's journey, and the connections that support and uplift your child and you just as you are. These bonds are different from your relationships before. They are forged through vulnerability, mutual understanding, and shared purpose. They remind you that you are not walking this path alone.

Awe: Strength That You Didn't Know Existed

Awe arrives when you witness your child's determination. It's in their refusal to give up, their resilience in the face of obstacles. It's also there in those moments when your child achieves something new or keeps up with an experience you weren't sure would be possible. Those moments pull at every heartstring and can truly take your breath away. Awe can also be directed inward—at yourself for what you've learned to carry, to navigate, and to overcome. You are doing things you never imagined you'd have to do. And that, too, is worthy of awe.

Peace: Finding Stillness in the Storm

Peace doesn't mean everything is okay. Instead, it means you've found a way to be okay with whatever is happening. It's the quiet moments when you stop fighting what is and find some form of acceptance. Peace comes in small doses at first: a few minutes of calm, a moment of clarity, or a deep breath that reaches your lungs. Gradually, it begins to show up more often, helping you navigate situations with more ease. Peace is not the absence of struggle but the presence of accepting what is alongside it.

EMBRACING YOUR EMOTIONAL JOURNEY

This journey isn't about fixing every feeling or being strong all the time. It's about learning to live with all your emotions with compassion and care. The goal isn't to eliminate difficult emotions, but to make space for all of them: the heavy and the light, the painful and the beautiful. Your feelings are signals guiding you toward what you need.

Let yourself feel what's true. You have survived 100 percent of your hardest days, and that is something to celebrate. You are not alone, and your emotions are valid. In time, as you learn to care for your own heart, you will begin to realize that your story doesn't exist in isolation. If you're in a partnership, the person beside you is also moving through their own experience of *The Thing*. Next, we will explore how two people, each navigating their own grief and emotions, can find their way through.

READER REFLECTION:
Honoring Your Emotions

Take a moment to sit with these questions. There are no right or wrong answers. Only your truth.

- Which emotions come up most easily when you think about your current emotional landscape?

- What emotions have felt the heaviest lately, and what might they be trying to tell you?

- Where do you feel safe exploring your emotions? When you're alone? With a loved one or a supportive professional?

- When was the last time a lighter emotion (like joy, peace, or gratitude) took center stage? How might you create more space for moments like this?

- When did you last allow yourself to simply feel without trying to fix or manage anything? What might it look like to give yourself permission to feel more often?

HEART-HOLDING PRACTICE
(FOR WHEN YOU NEED IT MOST)

This practice is for the tender moments. Come back to it whenever emotions feel heavy, confusing, or close to the surface. It can also meet you in lighter times when you just want to pause and examine what's here.

- **Notice what you're feeling right now.** Don't try to change it.

- **Name the feeling.** It might be sadness, guilt, frustration, love, pride, or joy.

- **Breathe.** Take a few slow, steady breaths. You are safe. What you are feeling is valid.

- **Be gentle.** Say something kind to yourself:

  » "This is hard, but I'm doing my best."

  » "This feels good, and I deserve to enjoy it."

You don't have to fix anything. Just hold what you feel with care. Even a few mindful breaths can be a small act of compassion.

AFFIRMATION

My emotions are messengers, not enemies.
They deserve my attention and compassion.

CHAPTER 4

Navigating Partnership

THE OTHER HALF OF THE JOURNEY

When two people come together in parenthood, they are called to face something complex. A journey full of love, growth, and learning to move through life as a team. When you add *The Thing*, the weight of everything amplifies. What we will explore next is what it looks like to navigate this journey alongside a partner: the hard conversations, the quiet disconnections, and the small ways two people can find their way back to each other. This isn't about a perfect partnership and having it all figured out. I'm going to share what I've learned in my own marriage when things felt impossibly hard, how to stay connected when everything feels heavy, and how to find your way back to each other when you've drifted apart.

THE SHARED CHALLENGES

Even the strongest partnerships are tested when special needs parenting enters the picture. This kind of parenting demands a transformation few are prepared for. You're asked to grow in directions you never imagined, often at different paces and in different ways. The roles you once knew, the rhythms you'd established, and the future you'd envisioned shifts.

But perhaps most challenging of all, this journey has a way of magnifying everything that was already there: the unresolved wounds, the communication patterns that weren't quite working, the different ways you handle stress, and the places where you felt unsupported, even before your child's diagnosis. Under this kind of pressure, small cracks can become deep divides. Old hurts resurface with new intensity. The issues you thought you'd moved past or learned to work around suddenly demand attention you don't have the energy to give.

Every partnership walks this journey differently. The emotional toll, the imbalance, and the strain land uniquely for each couple. Some grow stronger through the challenges. Others grow apart despite their best efforts. For many, it's a winding path of both: seasons of deep connection, followed by periods of distance while learning to love and support each other in entirely new ways. And sometimes, even with tremendous love and effort, the distance becomes too great to close. Some relationships shift beyond repair, despite everyone's best intentions. That doesn't mean failure, but it does mean change. And sometimes, change is the most loving choice for everyone involved. If your relationship shifts or ends during this journey, that's its own kind of strength. You're walking a different path, one filled with new-found courage and resilience. Your love for your child remains whole, and your capacity to nurture, advocate, and show up remains constant.

OUR STORY: WHEN EVERYTHING CHANGED

For my husband and me, the shift began as the "doing stage" intensified. Once the initial shock of *The Thing* wore off, we were left to figure out how to navigate this new reality. The diagnosis was vague and undefined, filled with unknowns. I couldn't sit in the ambiguity, so I threw myself into action. This included researching therapies, coordinating schedules, and becoming my child's advocate in every room we entered. My husband focused on what he knew best: logistics and financial security. He managed insurance battles, handled bills, and stayed on top of the day-to-day practicalities that kept our family running. What seemed like a natural division at first slowly became the beginning of an unintentional rift. I carried the emotional weight; he carried the logistical one. Both were essential acts of love, but instead of working together as a team, we grew defensive. Each of us was doing the best we could with the coping skills we had.

SAME STORM, DIFFERENT BOATS

We were weathering the same storm, but in completely different boats. I carried the emotional weight because I was physically present for the hardest moments: therapy sessions, watching our daughter struggle, and holding her through tears and frustration. Being her emotional anchor through each struggle left a residue that accumulated over time, settling in me like a slow, quiet grief. My husband managed everything else that kept our life running. Work, insurance, household logistics, and financial planning. The division made practical sense, but it meant our emotional experiences of our daughter's journey became vastly different.

How do you describe the weight of watching your child struggle through every milestone? How do you explain the hypervigilance that comes from being your child's emotional anchor? These experiences were mine alone to carry, and I didn't know how to translate them into words. Eventually, I stopped trying. Not because I believed he didn't care, but because I was too exhausted to bridge the gap.

WHEN PARENTING STYLES COLLIDE UNDER STRESS

What we didn't realize was how dramatically fear, stress, and untended emotions were affecting our parenting styles and emotional capacity. Under pressure, those styles became exaggerated and, sometimes, incompatible. I became hypervigilant and emotionally intense, researching every therapy option out there, advocating fiercely, staying constantly alert to her needs and progress. My stress response was to do more, know more, and ultimately, take more on myself if it could ease anything for my daughter. I believed that if I could just gather enough information and provide enough support, I could somehow protect her from any struggle. My husband's stress response was to focus and compartmentalize. His approach under pressure was to provide stability, stay busy in his own way, and preserve as much normalcy as possible.

Neither approach was wrong, but we were operating from completely different emotional capacities based on how much we were each carrying and how depleted we had become. I was in survival mode because I felt emotionally responsible for so many aspects of her journey. He was in survival mode because he felt practically responsible for keeping everything else functioning. What looked like different levels of caring was actually different ways of managing overwhelm. I interpreted his compartmentalization as emotional distance, and he interpreted my intensity as criticism of his approach. We were both drowning, but in completely different ways, and neither of us had the emotional bandwidth to recognize what was happening in the other.

WHEN LOVE MEETS CRISIS

Our marriage slipped into survival mode. We weren't growing apart out of indifference; we were drowning in separate storms, each fighting to keep our heads above water. There was no time or energy. In many seasons, we did not offer enough grace for each other. Our depletion made us defensive instead of curious. When you're running on empty, everything feels like a threat to your already fragile capacity—a suggestion feels like criticism, a different approach feels like judgment, and questions feel like attacks. We were both so depleted that we couldn't access the generosity and grace that could have made such a difference.

It wasn't one dramatic moment that broke our connection; it was the accumulation of countless small ones: unspoken frustrations, missed opportunities to truly see each other, and conversations that never happened because we were too depleted. We were both carrying enormous loads in different ways, and we didn't know how to meet in the middle. In the hardest moments, our relationship became a competition of who was more tired and who was carrying more. Resentment crept in. It was a defense mechanism when our frustration had nowhere else to go. Instead of bringing us closer, the very thing that should have united us was slowly dividing us. This is where the real disconnect happened. Not in the big fights, but in the daily loss of grace toward each other's different ways of coping with a difficult situation. We had also become disconnected from ourselves. And that's where the real healing had to begin.

THE CHOICE TO REBUILD

The turning point came through brutal honesty. I had to admit I was carrying too much and that I couldn't keep doing it alone. But I also had to recognize a painful truth: I had never fully let him in. I had built walls around my experience, assuming he couldn't understand, and then resented him for not understanding. So, I began there. I let him see the parts of me that were grieving and afraid. I stopped performing strength and started speaking my truth. And I had to pause long enough to really see him, too—as someone carrying his own stress and fears, someone who had his own way of coping.

We started therapy. Individually first, and then together. It gave us words for what had been buried: the grief we hadn't acknowledged, the imbalance we hadn't addressed, the fear of letting each other down. Some sessions were very difficult, but slowly, we began to soften toward each other. We started to see the hurt beneath the defensiveness, the tenderness beneath the walls. My turning point came when I realized I had to choose softness over being right. I had to understand that we both carried different stories and could only do our best from where we were. I needed to meet him where he was instead of where I wished he would be. If I wanted us to move forward together as a family, I had to make that choice consciously, daily, and sometimes, moment by moment. And in that softening, I opened up space for change. He became more open, more vulnerable, and more aware that he needed to understand his own emotional process as well.

SMALL STEPS, BIG CHANGES

We needed more than just time; we needed practices that brought us back to presence with ourselves and each other. I had started exploring mindfulness practices: sound baths, breathwork, and gentle spaces where my nervous system could finally soften. One day, I invited him to join me. To my surprise, he said yes. And even more surprising, he benefited from it. That shared stillness became an important space because it reminded us that presence and calm were something we could build together.

Connection didn't return dramatically. It came quietly, in shared silence that felt comfortable, in hugs that lasted longer, and in moments of genuine laughter that felt like relief. What helped us most wasn't one grand solution, but small, consistent choices requiring openness from both of us: honestly naming the roles we'd taken on, creating intentional moments of presence, eye contact during conversations, shared meals without distractions, and rediscovering laughter. We began making space for activities that filled us individually and as a couple. With time and intention, our marriage began to feel like a safe and familiar place again. Not because everything was resolved, but because we were actively choosing ourselves and consequently each other, one small act at a time.

WHAT THIS JOURNEY HAS TAUGHT US

Special needs parenting will stretch your partnership. It will deeply challenge you and force you to step into your greatest strengths as well as face your greatest weaknesses. In our case, our hardest moments forced us to realize that we needed to redefine and reestablish care—tender, consistent, intentional care. We had been moving through extraordinary stress without tending to ourselves or each other. We were both depleted and completely disconnected from our own needs. Over time, we learned to soften toward one another, to stop keeping score, to hold space for each other's process, even when it looked different from our own, and to recognize that both roles, emotional support and practical management, carry essential value. Sometimes, I carried more. Sometimes, he did. That rhythm kept shifting based on seasons and our individual capacity. What mattered most was being honest about where we were and how we could show up for each other from that place.

One of the greatest gifts was learning to see my husband not through my lens of exhaustion, but through compassion. He trusted me with the intimate details of our daughter's care. He held steady ground when I was falling apart. He coped differently, but he still felt deeply, worried constantly, and loved fiercely. He needed space and grace, too. Not just to help me, but to tend to his own emotional journey. And in this realization, I understood that partners need healing, too. They carry their own version of this journey, their own grief, and their own fears. While I fell apart outwardly, he was falling apart inwardly. He carried the same weight I did, but he expressed and processed it differently.

This emotional journey and the choice to prioritize healing belong to both. Partners deserve permission to feel deeply, to heal at their own pace, and to navigate their own version of this path. This is not just a mother's journey; it's a family journey. And everyone in the immediate circle deserves to be seen and honored in their own experience. They need spaces of vulnerability, support, connections, and tools that work for them. It shouldn't be exclusive to mothers or limited by gender. There's value in slowing down and honoring each person's journey, something that can be easier said than done, but it's worth considering. This goes for caregivers, siblings, and anyone in the inner circle, too. Through all of the tension, the growth, the learning to see each other with fresh eyes, there was one constant: our daughter's love. It was pure, constant, and unconditional. In many ways, it became the mirror that showed us how to love more patiently, more openly, and more fully.

WHERE WE ARE NOW

We still struggle, but have made the choice to grow together and not apart as we face life's challenges. We slip back into old patterns when we're depleted, but now, we're better equipped and more aware of the need to pause, check in with each other, and reset when necessary. We try to approach new challenges by being more careful to see the whole story and what each of us is carrying, rather than becoming defensive or making assumptions. This journey has changed us individually in ways we're still discovering. I'm not the same person as when *The Thing* first came into my life, and neither is he. We've developed new strengths, uncovered hidden emotions, and learned things about ourselves we never knew existed. Part of our work as a couple now is recognizing and respecting who we've each become, not just who we used to be together.

Sometimes, that means getting to know each other again. He has evolved through his own version of this experience. I've evolved, too. We're learning to see and appreciate these changes in each other, rather than expecting the familiar patterns of before. Some days, love feels more easily accessible, and we move toward each other with presence, grace, and acceptance. Other days, love feels harder. Sometimes, we choose self-protection. Sometimes, we need space to breathe and recenter until we're ready to connect. Sometimes, we choose silence when words feel too hard. Sometimes, we're too depleted to choose anything intentional at all, and we just survive the day. It's ongoing work, and some seasons are harder than others, but we keep showing up, imperfectly and with love. We've learned to recognize these rhythms as part of our story rather than evidence of failure.

COMMON RELATIONAL CHALLENGES

Every couple navigates this terrain differently, but there are common patterns that emerge. This path has a way of magnifying everything: the cracks and the strengths, the love and the stress, and what works beautifully and what falls apart under pressure. It creates significant challenges but also unique opportunities for deeper connection and intimacy.

Communication and Connection Gaps

- Transactional conversations that focus only on logistics, schedules, and immediate needs rather than emotional connection

- Communication gaps where assumptions fill the space that honest conversation should occupy

- Diminished intimacy due to chronic fatigue, stress, and the challenge of transitioning between caregiver and partner roles

Emotional and Practical Imbalances

- Resentment over unequal loads (emotional, physical, or mental) that builds slowly over time

- Different coping styles that can feel like abandonment or criticism, rather than complementary strengths

- Triggered childhood wounds or previous relationship injuries that resurface under stress

External Pressures

- Financial strain from therapies, specialists, medical bills, and lost income that creates additional pressure

- Family or cultural expectations that conflict with your child's needs or your reality

POTENTIAL SOURCES OF STRENGTH

Despite the challenges, this journey can also forge remarkable resilience and connection. A few of the ways my husband and I found strength were from:

Deepened Partnership

- New levels of resilience developed as a team through navigating challenges together

- Creative problem-solving skills and the joy of celebrating shared victories, no matter how small

Transformed Perspective

- Realignment of values and priorities that brings clarity about what truly matters

- Greater empathy and emotional depth that extends beyond our family into all relationships

IDEAS FOR RECONNECTION

Here are some gentle starting points that helped us rebuild our connection:

Communicate with Clarity and Compassion

- Ask for help specifically. Don't expect your partner to guess what you need. Be clear and direct about both practical and emotional support.

- Schedule honest check-ins. Set aside weekly time to talk about feelings, fears, and needs, not just logistics and schedules.

- Talk openly about this season. Have honest conversations about what you each need right now, acknowledging that those needs might be different from what they were before.

Create Intentional Connection

- Spend time together away from your child. Go for a walk, get coffee, or have a nice dinner. The goal is to be together as a couple and shed the parenting role for an hour or two.

- Inject joy intentionally. Laugh together. Be silly. Watch something funny. Listen to music you both love. Joy is a powerful healing force.

- Start small and be consistent. You don't need grand, romantic gestures; intentional moments of connection and presence are often more authentic and powerful.

Honor Your Differences

- Honor different coping styles. You don't have to process emotions the same way to support each other well. Learn to accept and appreciate, rather than judge your differences.

- Recognize that your strengths complement each other; you don't need to respond the same way to be on the same team.

THE INVITATION FORWARD

This chapter isn't about getting it all right. It's about showing up with presence and intention for the relationship you have. If your relationship feels strained, know that you're not alone. What matters most is how you choose to move forward from where you are right now. This journey asks for a new kind of partnership. One built on honesty, vulnerability, and deep compassion. You don't have to return to who you were as a couple before this began. In fact, you likely won't. But you can grow and evolve from exactly where you are today.

Each couple is unique. Take time to explore what "couple care" looks like for you now, not based on what your relationship was before, but honoring who you both are today and what you both need moving forward. Relationships evolve and change, so let yours become something new, something rooted in presence, shared humanity, and mindful love, rather than old expectations. Remember: You're not walking this path alone, and neither are they.

Just as partnerships evolve through this experience, so do all your other relationships. Family dynamics shift, sibling relationships become more complex, and friendships change in both challenging and unexpected ways. These shifting connections deserve their own exploration, understanding, and compassion.

READER REFLECTION:
Exploring Your Partnership

Take a moment to reflect on how your relationship has evolved and what you've learned together. These prompts are meant to help you notice both the challenges and the growth within your partnership and to discover new ways to nurture connection and understanding.

- How has your relationship with your partner changed since *The Thing* became part of your lives? What do you miss about how things once were? What do you now deeply appreciate?

- What unspoken roles have each of you taken on? Are those roles supporting your relationship or creating distance and imbalance?

- Do you feel that one of you is carrying more emotional weight right now? How can you find balance through empathy and shared care rather than comparison and resentment?

- What conversations have you been avoiding or postponing? What might it look like to create space for those talks in a safe, honest, and compassionate way?

- What small acts of connection can you bring back or try anew? Think beyond logistics: What helps you feel seen, and how can you offer that same presence to your partner?

AFFIRMATION

*Together, we're learning to grow with patience and grace.
I honor the different ways we love, and I trust that
our healing is unfolding, one moment at a time.*

CHAPTER 5

Shifts in Connections

BEYOND THE DIAGNOSIS: HOW RELATIONSHIPS CHANGE

If you've noticed that some of your relationships feel different now (warmer in some cases, more distant in others), then you're not alone. Parenting, and in this case, special-needs parenting, creates profound changes that ripple outward, touching connections in ways you might not have expected. This isn't something to fear, though it can feel overwhelming at first. It's an inevitable process where some connections will grow stronger while others may quietly fade. It becomes obvious who shows up with genuine support and who feels uncertain about how to walk alongside you. Through it all, you'll discover something profound about yourself: what you are willing to accept and what you are ready to leave behind with care and gratitude for what it was, while honoring the life you have now.

THE COMPLEXITY OF PERSONAL CHANGE

Even when you have steady support, the overall nature of connection becomes more complex. Your energy has shifted. Your priorities have crystallized. When your emotional bandwidth narrows and your time becomes more precious, what and who you give it to naturally begins to change. But here's what I didn't expect: Sometimes, the distance I felt wasn't because people were pulling away from me. Sometimes, it was because I was changing, and that made it hard to figure out what was really happening.

I've been incredibly fortunate to have steady support from my family and close friends. They showed up from day one and never stopped. They didn't offer answers or solutions; instead, they gave me their presence. And yet, even surrounded by all that support, I often felt profoundly alone. Looking back, I realize that while a lot of my support system remained consistent, I was changing. In my hardest seasons, I was more sensitive, more overwhelmed, and often more withdrawn. In that state, even the most familiar relationships felt different. Much of what I experienced was filtered through exhaustion, fear, and emotional fog.

Sometimes, I didn't want solutions or encouragement. Sometimes, I didn't even want company. I just wanted space to be in it, to sit with the weight of it, to fall apart without having to explain why or reassure anyone that I'd be okay. In those moments, I was caught between two realities: the loving people around me who wanted to help, and my own raw need to simply exist in the difficulty without pretending to be okay for anyone else. I felt guilty for not being able to receive their care in the way they were offering it, yet I also felt protective of my right to feel everything fully without having to manage other people's discomfort with my pain.

This dynamic created distance even with people who weren't going anywhere. The relationships themselves weren't changing, but my capacity to engage with them was. I was learning that, sometimes, the shifts we experience in our connections aren't about others pulling away or failing to understand. Sometimes, they're about us needing something different than what we've always needed. Understanding this difference became crucial because it helped me sort through what was happening around me: which relationship changes were about other people's discomfort or inability to adapt, and which were simply about my own changing needs. Both are real, but they require different responses.

THE UNEXPECTED REORDERING

As you change, you'll notice that some relationships shift in ways you didn't anticipate. Sometimes, the support you expected doesn't show up. The family member who seemed understanding becomes distant when your child's needs become more visible. The friend who promised to be there disappears when things get complicated. And then there are the comments. Oh, the comments. Ever heard these?

- "Have you tried cutting out gluten? I read somewhere that diet can cure these things in kids."

- "Well, at least your child is high functioning."

- "God only gives special children to special parents."

- "Everything happens for a reason."

These well-meaning words can land heavily, causing anger, resentment, and even a desire to shut certain people out of your life. They often come from people who may genuinely care about you, people trying to help or offer comfort. Yet, they often leave you feeling more alone than if they had said nothing at all. The family member who casually suggests over dinner that maybe if you just changed your child's diet and cut back on-screen time, they'd "grow out of it." The one who later pulls you aside and tells you you're being "too dramatic" about your child's needs, stating that all kids develop at their own pace. The friend who stops inviting you to gatherings. When you finally ask about it, she hesitates, stumbles over her words, then quietly admits she thought it might be "too much" for your child. In those moments, you realize that some people aren't equipped to walk alongside you in this journey. Not because they're bad people, but because they can't stretch beyond their own understanding or comfort zone.

FAMILY CONNECTIONS

Family can be where some of the most powerful and, sometimes, painful shifts happen. These are the people who knew you before, who have been there since your child arrived in this world, and who sometimes have the hardest time understanding that everything is different now. These disconnections hurt in a different way because of all the history and trust there. When family members struggle to accept your child or your new reality, it's not just about losing support. You're also losing the people you expected to walk beside you, especially during this journey.

But not all family members react this way. The family members who do show up become essential. Their presence doesn't eliminate the hard parts, but it makes everything so much more manageable. And that genuine love and support, offered without judgment, can feel like everything. Some family members and good friends can become what I've come to think of as fairy godmothers. These are the ones who embrace your new reality without hesitation. The people who learn your child's language and celebrate their wins as their own. They don't just tolerate your child's differences; they genuinely appreciate them. They see past the struggles to recognize your child's unique gifts and help you see them, too.

SIBLINGS: THE GENTLE CARRIERS

If you have other children, it adds another layer of complexity. These little ones are experiencing their own version of this journey, watching, adapting, and carrying more than we sometimes realize. We welcomed our son two years after our daughter was born. Even before he had words to express it, I could see the quiet ways he adapted: his empathy bloomed early, he picked up on cues with remarkable ease, he intuitively understood that our family's rhythm was different than other families he'd been around, and he adjusted accordingly.

Siblings of children with special needs often carry more than we realize. They can experience a full spectrum of emotions: pride, confusion, protectiveness, frustration, and resentment. All of it is valid. All of it is real. Their questions will come. Honest and curious questions about why things work differently in your family. These conversations deserve honesty rather than deflection, and age-appropriate explanations that honor all your children's experiences. They will also witness the ignorant comments and awkward moments from outsiders. They see the stares at the playground. They hear the comments from other kids who don't understand. Sometimes, they become fierce protectors, and sometimes, they feel embarrassed or unsure. All these responses are normal and deserve space, support, and guidance.

THE BALANCING ACT

Beyond the sibling path, there's the internal struggle that comes for a parent or caregiver with multiple children. All parents wrestle with dividing attention and meeting different needs, but when one child requires significant extra support, there's another layer of complexity that can add guilt to everyday life. I've spent countless days feeling pulled in opposite directions. I'm often torn between two children I love desperately. I've worried I was failing one while trying to support the other. That guilt lingered like a shadow. But over time, I've learned to meet those moments with grace instead of shame. Grace has looked like carving out small pockets of uninterrupted time with each child. With my son, it may be ten minutes of reading together before bed. With my daughter, it can look like going to the park and playing her favorite game. These intentional moments have become essential for them and for me. They allow me to connect deeply with each child, to witness their unique personalities, and to tend to their individual worlds.

What I've noticed through our journey is how my son has become his sister's greatest champion. He's naturally mindful about meeting her where she is, while she's always thinking of him. Of course, they still have typical sibling moments, but watching them together reminds me that what matters most isn't doing everything perfectly; it's about showing up with love and making sure they both know they're seen and valued for who they are.

I am also more mindful of the environment I create at home. When I feel like I'm about to lose it, I pause and breathe. Not to pretend everything's fine when it's not, but to keep from adding my own chaos to whatever is already happening. This approach respects each child's needs and prevents me from creating additional stress for both. I've learned that stress feeds off stress, so I'm mindful about not overreacting and keeping disagreements or my own stress to a minimum, especially in front of my kids. It's important not to add unnecessary tension to our home environment.

THE EVOLUTION OF FRIENDSHIP

Friendships don't always survive the profound shift that comes with special needs parenting. Some people simply can't bridge the gap because they haven't lived the emotional weight, the daily unpredictability, or the long-term uncertainties you now carry. You see it happening in the friend who stops calling because she doesn't know what to say. The well-meaning mom who says, "I don't know how you do it," as if you had a choice. Sometimes, I found myself outgrowing relationships that once felt important but no longer aligned with the life I was living. That gap can create distance that hurts. It can feel isolating to realize that relationships you thought were solid weren't built to weather this kind of change. There's real grief in recognizing that certain connections may fade or no longer fit, but it also reveals what's real.

Some friendships grow deeper under pressure. The ones who stay, who check in without expecting immediate responses, who listen without needing the full story, who sit beside you without trying to fix anything—those are your people. These are the friends who text "Thinking of you" without needing a reply, who show up with coffee without being asked, who remember the difficult appointments and follow up afterward, and who genuinely celebrate your child's milestones, however small they might seem to the outside world.

THE WORKPLACE AND
EXTENDED SOCIAL CIRCLES

Your professional relationships and broader social circles will also feel the ripple effects. Colleagues may struggle to understand why you need flexibility for appointments or why certain workplace events no longer work for your family. Some will surprise you with their understanding and support, while others may view your new reality as an inconvenience. Extended social circles (the parents from school, neighbors, and acquaintances from various activities) often reveal their true nature during this time. Some will step forward with unexpected kindness, while others may fade into polite distance. I've learned that not every relationship needs to be deep or life changing. Some connections serve different purposes, and that's okay. What matters is knowing which relationships deserve your emotional energy and which ones you can keep at a comfortable surface level.

UNEXPECTED CONNECTIONS

New friendships can often bloom in surprising places: therapy waiting rooms, support groups, or brief conversations with someone who simply welcomes you and your child with genuine interest and acceptance. I've formed unexpected connections in unlikely settings, such as the mom I met while our kids were in therapy together. At first, it was just a smile in the waiting room, but over time, it became a shared space for resources, connection, and understanding. Not because our children have similar diagnoses, but because we recognized something in each other. These connections aren't built on convenience or proximity. They're built on shared truth. They offer understanding instead of pity. They welcome you and your story exactly as you are. These are the people who get it when you say your child had a good day because it means something completely different than it might for other families.

LEARNING TO COMMUNICATE YOUR NEEDS AND SET BOUNDARIES

I realized that part of moving forward and doing what was best for my family and me meant equipping myself with better tools and new ways of setting appropriate boundaries. This is where finding your voice and communicating your needs becomes crucial.

- "Please don't try to fix this. Just be with me in it."

- "I'm not looking for advice. I just need you to listen."

- "I know this might not make sense, but this is what I need right now."

Learning to be direct takes time and practice, but when you become clearer about what you need, people can show up in more meaningful ways. I also learned to address unhelpful comments head-on, gently but firmly:

- "I appreciate the thought, but her team of specialists already has a treatment plan in place."

- "I know you're trying to help, but comments like that can feel isolating when you're living this every day."

Most of the time, people respond with understanding when you give them the chance to do better. And in situations where communication isn't enough, and they are not respectful of your needs and wishes, that also tells you something important about that relationship. In that case, a stronger boundary may need to be set, and your connection with that person may need to be limited or paused for that season of your life.

REDEFINING CONNECTION

Connection looks different for me now. It requires a quieter, more intentional kind of effort. Not the kind that leaves me drained, but the kind that nourishes me. Even something as simple as memes and messages have become meaningful forms of connection. People send me memes during hard periods. Some are funny and some are profound, but both mean a lot. Those little bursts of humor and connection become tiny lifelines, reminders that someone was thinking of me.

I no longer stretch myself thin to maintain relationships that feel one-sided or misaligned with the life I'm living now. It's painful to recognize that certain connections may fade or no longer fit, but there's also freedom in accepting those shifts with honesty and compassion, for them and for myself. I treasure the people who continue to show up with gentleness and presence. The friends who don't need me to be okay all the time, who ask, "How can I be here for you today?"

Friendship in this season isn't about quantity, but about depth. It's about people who can meet you where you are, walk beside you, and hold space for your life, even when their own looks completely different. Most importantly, I'm learning to extend that same grace to myself—to honor my need for solitude, to choose rest over conversation when I need it, and to remind myself that it's okay to evolve. It's okay to change. And it's okay to let go of what no longer fits.

THE INVITATION FORWARD

Relationships will shift. Some will deepen, some may fall away, and others will surprise you with their quiet strength. Letting go doesn't always mean loss. Sometimes, it's an opening, an invitation for peace, clarity, and connections that feel more aligned with the life you're living now. Find your tribe, the ones who show up, who stay, and who hold space for both the mess and the magic. Those are your people. Keep nurturing those bonds. But remember to begin with the one that matters most: the relationship you have with yourself. And it starts by exploring how you care for and nurture your own well-being.

READER REFLECTION:
Navigating Shifts in Relationships

As your journey unfolds, so will your connections. You'll grieve some, you'll fight for others, and some will grow in ways you never expected. These prompts are here to help you reflect on those shifts with honesty, gentleness, and compassion for the person you're becoming.

- **Changing relationships:** Which connections have shifted the most over time, especially since this journey began? Have any grown distant, surprised you, or changed in unexpected ways?

- **Your fairy godmothers:** Who has become a lifeline for you in this season? What are you most grateful for in their support? (Remember, even a small thank-you or letting them know how much you appreciate them can mean everything.)

- **If you have other children:** How has this journey shaped their experience? What do you hope they know, feel, or understand about their sibling and about their own place in your family?

- **Seeking understanding:** Is there someone you wish understood your journey more fully? What would you want to say to them if you could speak freely from your heart?

- **Boundaries:** Have you encountered comments or reactions that didn't feel supportive? How did you respond, and what might you do differently to protect your peace?

AFFIRMATION

I give myself permission to grow through change.
Even as my relationships shift, I remain rooted in love.
I honor what is true and release what no longer fits.
I trust that new forms of connection
can bloom in their own time.

CHAPTER 6

Claiming Self-Care

RECLAIMING WHAT WAS NEVER A LUXURY

Self-care gets tossed around like it's a luxury. People think of self-care in terms of spa days, bubble baths, or something to treat yourself to when life slows down. But when you're parenting a child with special needs, self-care is survival. It's the foundation of your relationship with yourself and the heartbeat of your ability to sustain the one you have with your child. Self-care isn't about waiting for the to-do list to end. It's about sending your body a message: *You matter, too.* Not someday. Now. Everything we explore on this journey (resilience, acceptance, advocacy, and community) rests on one vital truth: You cannot pour from an empty cup. You cannot show up fully for your child if you're constantly abandoning yourself. You know the airplane instruction: Put your oxygen mask on first. Not because you're selfish, but because the survival of your kids demands it. Parenting requires breath. So does healing. So does love. And yet, so many of us live like we're holding our breath.

THE MYTH THAT KEEPS US STUCK

Parenting a child with special needs reshapes you in every way. Your energy, your identity, and your bandwidth are constantly challenged through appointments, advocacy, exhaustion, and emotional weight. Your own needs slip quietly to the bottom of the list. You tell yourself, "I'll rest after the IEP issue is resolved. After the insurance battle. After everything else." But there's always something else. And here's the myth so many of us live under: *Taking care of myself means taking something away from my child.* We confuse self-sacrifice with love. We equate rest with weakness. We wear exhaustion like a badge of honor. But depletion doesn't serve anyone. Your stress becomes your family's stress. Your overwhelm ripples outward. Your capacity to be with yourself and others shrinks. Your spark dims. The question shouldn't be, "Do I have time for self-care?" but "Why don't I believe I deserve it?"

WHAT BURNOUT REALLY LOOKS LIKE

I lived under this self-sacrifice myth for years. I believed that self-care was something to squeeze in only after everything else was taken care of. A quick coffee run, an occasional bath, a rushed meetup with a friend … all small moments I tried to claim after the real work was done. But underneath was an exhaustion and disconnect that couldn't be repaired by these quick breaks. What I needed was much bigger than these small moments of relief. The truth is that burnout doesn't announce itself with a clear diagnosis. Instead, it creeps in gradually, showing up in ways we often dismiss or push through. It wears many faces:

- **Physical:** sleep issues, chronic tension, fatigue you can't shake, immune system on edge. Your body starts holding all the stress in your shoulders, your back, and your jaw. Even when you have the chance to rest, you can't seem to recover.

- **Mental:** brain fog, forgetfulness, scattered thoughts, decision paralysis. You lose your keys constantly, forget appointments, and struggle with simple decisions. Your brain feels like a computer with too many tabs open. Everything is slow, and nothing processes clearly.

- **Emotional:** anxiety, numbness, irritability, sadness, disconnection from joy or self. You snap at people you love over small things, or you feel completely numb to things that used to bring you happiness. You cry over small things, or you can't cry at all, even when you desperately need to.

For me, the wake-up call came when I realized I couldn't answer basic questions about myself anymore. I couldn't remember what I loved, what I needed, or who I was beyond being a "special-needs mom" and going through the motions of adulting. I was simply managing and surviving, but not living or thriving. That realization became a turning point.

THE SHIFT THAT CHANGED EVERYTHING

I used to believe self-care had to be big: a full day off or a trip away. But when those weren't possible, I was left doing nothing. I waited for time to magically appear, and it never did. My breaking point forced a shift in my entire way of thinking about myself and my self-care. Eventually, I started asking myself different questions. I stopped asking, "What more can I give?" and started asking, "What do I need to keep giving with love?" I stopped wondering, "Can I make time for self-care?" and began asking, "How do I make it nonnegotiable?" I stopped questioning, "What is selfish?" and began to ask, "What is sacred?" My self-care didn't begin with spa days; it began with five minutes.

- Drinking coffee before anyone else woke up

- A quick stretch routine before bed

- A deep breath in my car before going inside

- Catching a glimpse of a sunrise

- A moment with myself after bedtime

These moments weren't big, but they became anchoring ways I worked self-care into my daily life.

EXPLORING SELF-CARE

Self-care isn't about escaping your life. It's about returning to yourself within it. It's about being present with your own body, your own breath, and your own needs, even in the middle of the chaos. Real self-care is simply doing something, anything, that helps you feel more grounded, supported, or lighter. At its core, it requires presence and pause. Moments where you can remember that your needs matter, too. Self-care should be preventive, not just reactive. It's what you do to maintain your well-being, not something to help you recover from depletion. Think of it like taking vitamins or making healthy lifestyle choices, rather than waiting until you're sick to take medicine. It's about caring for yourself before your system starts struggling.

Self-care is also personal and flexible. What nourishes you may drain someone else, and what works in one season of your life may not work in another. It's small and sustainable because consistency matters more than grand gestures. There's a common phrase I've heard from many parents, especially special needs parents: "I would die for my child." And while the sentiment is understandable, I've also heard professionals challenge this notion with a powerful question: "But why wouldn't you live for your child?" This reframing is where your self-care plan comes into play. Living for your child means being present and sustained enough to walk alongside them instead of sacrificing yourself. The goal isn't to create the ideal routine or do everything "right." The goal is to listen to your body, your emotions, and your deepest needs, and then respond with care.

WORKING THROUGH COMMON OBSTACLES

Even when we understand that self-care is essential, we still run into barriers. Working through these obstacles isn't about getting it right; it's about awareness. And once we name what stands in our way, we can begin to choose differently—slowly, gently, and in ways that honor the season we're in. That awareness is what helped me take my first real steps toward caring for myself again.

- **"I don't have time."** Some seasons are brutally busy. Medical appointments, hospital stays, regressions, and being in survival mode. In those seasons, five minutes of intentional breathing can be incredibly powerful. Self-care doesn't have to be lengthy to be effective.

- **"I can't afford it."** You don't need to spend money to carve out some time for yourself. Some of my most healing moments came from a walk around the block, a journaling session accompanied by a supportive and calming candle, and even five minutes of silence. Libraries, You-Tube, and apps offer free or low-cost resources. Be creative.

- **"I'm being selfish."** This belief runs deep, but what message are we giving our children if they see us constantly abandoning ourselves? We model for them what self-care looks like, and this practice starts with how we treat ourselves.

- **"No one sees how much I need this."** Sometimes, you must name it clearly. Not, "I need a break," but, "I need thirty minutes alone so I can face the bedtime routine with patience." Be specific. Be honest. Educate the people around you when needed.

- **"This won't change anything."** Sometimes, we delay self-care because we're afraid. We fear it won't help, won't change our situation, or that we're beyond repair. But sometimes, we make excuses because caring for ourselves takes us out of familiar patterns of neglect that, while painful, often feel comfortable. Start so small you can't fail: one deep breath, a small thing that is just for you, or one kind word.

- **"People will judge me."** Some might, especially when they see you choosing to make yourself a priority, but self-care isn't about their opinions; it's about how you want to feel in your own life. Seek out the ones who cheer you on, not the ones who question your worthiness. Surround yourself with people who understand that your well-being matters, not just for you, but for everyone you love.

MY VERSION OF SELF-CARE

When I started exploring my emotional world and giving myself permission to factor *me* back in, I began to see how essential self-care really was. What followed wasn't a single breakthrough, but an evolution: small, intentional choices that helped me feel alive again, one moment at a time. Some of my self-care practices were traditional and familiar: movement, personal care, and quiet spaces. Others might seem less conventional, yet they're part of a growing awareness around holistic wellness, an approach that invites us to integrate all parts of who we are.

What struck me most about many of these practices was the invitation to turn inward and share with vulnerability, while being gently held in that space. They stood in stark contrast to the frantic rhythm of survival mode that I had been living in, and the outside noise that can be overwhelming and unsupportive. These practices created room for calm, quiet environments where I could finally tune into my body, hear my breath, and feel my own heartbeat. I needed that stillness to remind my nervous system that there was another way to live, that safety and softness were possible.

Over time, I also noticed that the biggest obstacle wasn't time or circumstance; it was often myself. Guilt whispered that I didn't deserve to feel good, that I was too old to dance freely, that life was too hard and serious for joy and play. I told myself I didn't have time, that caring for myself would take away from "more important" things. Learning to notice and gently challenge those beliefs became part of the healing itself. Because self-care wasn't just about what I *did*; it was about remembering that I was worthy of the same care and tenderness I so freely gave to everyone else.

RECONNECTING WITH JOY
(LIFE DOESN'T HAVE TO BE SO SERIOUS)

Joy didn't come rushing back all at once—it returned in small, honest ways. For a while, I was carrying so much that I forgot what it felt like to enjoy myself without overthinking it. Little by little, I started inviting moments of lightness back in, not to escape my life, but to remember there was more to me than the hard parts. Here are a few things that helped me remember what joy feels like:

- **Dancing around my house:** I didn't need special choreography. I moved because it felt good. Dancing helped me remember that my body wasn't just a vessel for carrying stress and responsibilities. It could also be a source of joy and expression. Some days, that meant slow music for gentle movement. Other days, I blasted "Unwritten" to remind myself that our story was still being written. And on some days, I listened to reggaeton to really get me moving. (The Latina in me me needed to dance it out. Dont' Judge.)

- **Using my voice freely:** I sang dramatic ballads in the car. Other times, I sang silly songs with my kids. When I was feeling more at ease, I would hum to hear my voice and get centered.

- **Creating by picking up art projects, writing, or crafts:** Even if I wasn't great at a specific craft, I tried it anyway to feel alive, and it connected me to old or new parts of myself.

- **Speaking kind words and affirmations to myself in the mirror:** Looking at myself in the mirror felt ridiculous at first, but it became surprisingly healing. I realized that so many times, we fear what's in the mirror, but learning to be present with ourselves while making eye contact is where real connection begins.

Tending to My Body

- **Exercising in ways that felt good:** This became an essential practice. I did yoga when I needed deep stretching and to feel grounded. I did more intense exercise when I needed greater release. I found somatic movement helpful when I needed to reconnect more deeply with my body. I discovered that movement wasn't about punishment or achieving some ideal body; it was about honoring what my body needed in that moment.

- **Drinking water regularly:** This sounds so basic, but I realized I was chronically dehydrated from constantly tending to everyone else's needs and drinking too much caffeine. Making sure I drank water throughout the day became an act of self-care.

- **Eating real meals, not leftovers:** This meant sitting down to eat instead of finishing my kids' leftovers. It meant planning meals that nourished me, not just filled my stomach.

- **Basic grooming that made me feel good:** I scheduled regular nail appointments, haircuts, and whatever made me feel better about myself. These were ways of saying, "I matter enough to take care of."

- **Choosing comfort:** I chose soft clothes that felt good against my skin, warm baths that weren't rushed, and gentle touch through a massage or even just putting on lotion mindfully.

- **Prioritizing rest over scrolling:** My nervous system needs actual rest, not the false stimulation of social media. So, when it's time for bed, I try not to bring the phone with me.

Clearing the Mental Clutter

- **Journaling became a brain dump:** This practice requires no fancy prompts or perfect prose, just allowing everything swirling in my head to transfer onto paper. Sometimes, I made angry scribbles. Sometimes, gratitude lists. Sometimes, a feelings map to track what I was experiencing. The format didn't matter; the release did.

- **Five-minute meditations:** You can do this with meditation apps, YouTube videos, or guided meditations. These were usually short enough that I couldn't make excuses. I started with guided meditations because my mind was too scattered for silence, but those five minutes taught me I could find stillness and breath even in chaos.

- **Saying no more often:** This was a revolutionary form of self-care. I had to learn that saying no to one thing meant saying yes to something else (usually my own well-being).

- **Turning off notifications:** This small action gave my nervous system permission to stop being on high alert constantly. The world didn't end when I wasn't immediately available to every text and email.

- **Therapy, even while sitting in my car:** Sometimes, the only private space I could find for a therapy session was in my car, but those sessions became lifelines.

Creating Soothing Spaces

- **Lighting a candle:** I did this to honor a moment for myself. Sometimes, it was while reading, journaling, tidying the house, or simply sitting still, watching the flame and enjoying its pleasant scent.

- **Keeping one uncluttered corner that felt like mine:** It became a ritual to dedicate a calm and peaceful space for just myself. Having this area signaled to my body: *This is safe and just mine.* It made a surprising difference in my nervous system.

- **Setting the mood with music:** Sometimes, I would play an uplifting song. Other times, I chose acoustic or instrumental music when I needed calm. It became about listening to what my body was craving in that moment.

- **Sitting outside, even for a few minutes:** This helped me remember there was a world beyond our immediate struggles. Fresh air and natural light became medicine.

Letting Go

- **Crying after hard appointments:** This release became acceptable instead of something I had to hide or feel ashamed about. Those tears allowed me to process difficult emotions.

- **Screaming into a pillow or aloud:** On a few occasions, I screamed out loud with a group of strangers at workshops or retreats. Other times, when I was on my own, either out loud, in my car, or at home. It felt very strange at first, but it was incredibly liberating and gave my anger and big emotions a safe way out.

- **Decluttering to release stuck energy:** This became my go-to practice when emotions felt too big for my body. There's something powerful about clearing external chaos when everything inside feels overwhelming. (Decluttering can also symbolically mean you are getting rid of things that no longer serve you and opening space for things that you need and are ready for.)

Trying New (Spiritual-ish) Practices

- **Breathwork:** A few deep breaths could anchor my body and calm my nervous system in minutes. These intentional breaths became more powerful than I expected. Paying attention to my breath for a few minutes could shift my entire emotional state.

- **Following moon phases as check-in points:** The moon offered me a gentle rhythm for self-reflection. New moons are for setting intentions. Full moons are for releasing what no longer serves you. This felt like having a natural timer for emotional maintenance.

- **Drawing affirmation or oracle cards:** These cards provided gentle daily guidance and reminded me that I deserved encouragement and support, even if it was from myself.

- **Reiki, sound healing, and hypnosis:** These modalities opened me up to healing approaches I'd never considered. Receiving energetic support to help move heavy or stagnant energy, sound bowls, gongs, rain sticks, chimes, or guided meditations to reach a deep meditative state became tools for accessing deeper states of relaxation and understanding.

- **Creating a small space with meaningful items:** I chose photos, small items, and books that reminded me of strength and promoted calmness. This gave me a visual nudge that my spiritual well-being mattered, too.

PERMISSION TO BLOOM

One of the most important experiences in my journey was a half-day women's retreat called Bloom. I nearly didn't go. The familiar guilt about taking time away from my family whispered its usual concerns: the expense, the voice that said I didn't deserve it, that it wouldn't change anything, but something deeper pulled me there.

The day included breathwork, meditation, sound healing, and movement. But more than the techniques, it offered me permission to simply *be* without fixing, solving, or performing. The retreat gave me something I hadn't experienced in years: the space to be present with myself without agenda or expectation. I was also able to let go and let joy in, even if only for a little while. It was a chance to connect, to be supported, and to remember what it feels like to care for and love myself.

During the breathwork, I felt my nervous system begin to calm for the first time in months. The sound healing helped me access a stillness I'd forgotten. Through sound, I was simply receiving care instead of giving it. When the movement portion began, I froze. A lot of the women were dancing freely. Normally, I love music and dancing, but in that moment, I just stood there, stiff and self-conscious. After a few minutes, I slowly started to sway my body, and in that tiny movement, something shifted. First came tears, then laughter, and finally, relief.

In that small, hesitant motion, something inside me cracked wide open. Years of held tension, unexpressed grief, and suppressed joy came flooding out. I remember thinking to myself, *Why am I withholding something so simple from myself? Why the punishment? Why do I believe I don't deserve to be here and feel joy?* That moment took me back to myself, to the me who loves to dance but had been buried under years of survival, fear, and guilt. Joy, playfulness, and ease rose back up for me to feel them. Not someday when everything was "handled," but right now. I was reminded that making self-care a priority didn't diminish what I could give my children. It enhanced it. It would give them a mother who was more present, more joyful, and more whole.

THE RIPPLE EFFECT

When you care for yourself:

- Your child receives a more grounded, emotionally-available parent.

- Your partner gets more connection, not just survival.

- Your other children experience more joy in the home.

- You remember who you are.

- You get to model something powerful for your children: Every person deserves care, and this includes you.

WHEN SELF-CARE DEEPENS

As you begin to feel more grounded and connected through these foundational practices, something beautiful may arise. You may find yourself naturally craving something deeper. Once the immediate overwhelm starts to ease, you may want self-care that goes beyond just managing stress. You crave practices that help you connect more deeply with yourself and build a foundation that can carry you through this entire journey. This is the natural evolution of caring for yourself. As your foundation strengthens, so does your capacity for deeper healing and transformation.

When you're ready to move beyond temporary relief and into practices that will truly sustain you and bring you closer to yourself, deeper self-care awaits. Next, we'll explore the next layer of healing that helped me: four doorways to a deeper kind of understanding that transforms not just how you cope, but how you move toward greater peace and acceptance of yourself and your journey.

READER REFLECTION:
The Invitation Forward

Start small, and remember that you are a person who is whole, worthy, and allowed to feel good. Let this chapter be a turning point, a gentle reminder of who you are beneath it all. Self-care is deeply personal. What nourishes you may look different from what nourishes someone else. The key is to start where you are, with what you have, and build from there.

ASSESS WHERE YOU ARE NOW

Take an honest look at your current relationship with self-care.

- What does self-care currently look like in your life? Is it something you practice regularly, or something you tell yourself you'll get to *someday?*

- What emotions come up when you think about prioritizing yourself? Guilt, relief, resistance, fear, comfort? These feelings are valuable information.

- What gets in the way of caring for yourself? Time, lack of support, low motivation, or beliefs about what makes you a "good parent"?

CHOOSE YOUR STARTING POINT

Pick one small act of self-care you could realistically do in the next week, and later build on that. The goal is to keep it simple and doable. You don't want to add more overwhelm or set yourself up for something that doesn't fit your life right now.

- Take a ten-minute walk around the block.

- Drink your coffee slowly, without multitasking.

- Go to bed thirty minutes earlier.

- Take three deep breaths before responding to a challenging moment.

- Listen to a favorite song and move freely if it feels right.

CREATE YOUR GENTLE PLAN

If it feels manageable, choose one practice from each area:

- **Care for your body:** Move in ways that feel good, improve your sleep, eat nourishing food, or simply drink more water.

- **Support your emotional well-being:** Journal, meditate, talk to a therapist, practice breathwork, or list things you're grateful for.

- **Nurture joy and connection:** Enjoy music, creativity, laughter, time with people who energize you, or moments of play.

Write them somewhere to serve as gentle reminders of how you want to care for yourself. The goal isn't perfection; it's presence. You're creating a foundation of care that can bend on hard days and grow on easier ones. You can be both a devoted parent and a person who deserves rest, joy, and kindness. Taking care of yourself isn't selfish; it shows your children what it means to value yourself as a whole person.

AFFIRMATION

*Self-care is my anchor, the place I return to refill
my cup so I can care for everyone else.
I challenge feelings of guilt because I am
also worthy of care and love.*

CHAPTER 7

Deeper Self-Care, Reimagined

THE QUIET AWAKENING

There's a moment that arrives quietly, and often unexpectedly. Maybe it's during a brief pause between the endless demands, or in those rare minutes when the world finally goes still. You feel something stirring that's different from the usual scramble for quick relief. It's deeper than that. A gentle but persistent ache that whispers, "This isn't enough anymore."

You're no longer just trying to escape or survive until bedtime. Something in you is asking to be remembered, to be found again—it's the part of you that exists beyond the constant responding, the perpetual doing, and the endless giving of yourself. In these stolen pockets of quiet, you begin to hear yourself again. *Really* hear yourself. You notice the difference between reacting from a place of depletion and choosing your response. Between pushing through another day and truly inhabiting it.

You might find yourself thinking something that feels both foreign and familiar: *My well-being matters. I miss who I am beneath it all.* This recognition is significant. You're not just looking for better coping strategies anymore. You're beginning to sense that there might be a different way to live within your own life. A way that doesn't require you to disappear in your own life while you are showing up for everything else. The longing you feel is valuable insight. Your deeper self is finally getting your attention.

WHEN SELF-CARE TRANSFORMS

This is where self-care transforms from a to-do list item into a way of being. Where it stops being about squeezing in moments of escape and becomes about fundamentally changing how you move through your days. Eventually, you may start wondering, *What would it feel like to enjoy my body again instead of just pushing through it each day? What emotions have I been too busy to feel or have been avoiding? When did I stop trusting my own instincts? What would happen if I let myself want something just for me?* These questions don't come with easy answers, but they point toward something that goes beyond bubble baths or some occasional "me" time. They require a more intentional practice of turning inward long enough to remember who you are and who you're becoming beneath all the roles you play.

THE JOURNEY BACK TO MYSELF

Through my own process of unraveling and rediscovering, I found that coming back to myself wasn't about becoming someone new. It was about remembering who I was and integrating who I was becoming.

It meant walking through different layers of healing that helped me release what had quietly accumulated over time. During the hardest seasons of this journey, I became deeply disconnected from myself. So many unfamiliar emotions and fears I never expected to carry made me feel like a stranger in my own life: the exhaustion, the constant vigilance, the pressure to do more, the judgment I placed on myself for not being enough, and the habit of putting everyone else's needs before my own. In this stressful state of being, I developed protective layers.

Those layers had served me when life felt too heavy, but as I began this deeper work, I realized they were also keeping me from myself. It began with recognizing the story my body had been holding—the tension, the fatigue, and the memories it had quietly stored. As I started to reconnect with my body, I could finally access the deeper layers beneath it all. My healing unfolded across four main areas: physical, emotional, spiritual, and soulful. Over time, they began to weave together, moving in rhythm, each one supporting and guiding the others.

MY FOUR DOORWAYS

Physical Care: Creating Safety in Your Own Skin

My body had become a home for years of accumulated stress and unexpressed emotions, with nowhere to go. For years, I felt like a rusty engine that had forgotten how to move, often lacking the fuel to get going. But my body was asking for something deeper than just movement. It needed to feel safe. It needed ways to release what I'd been holding inside. It needed to feel grounded.

When the tension and heaviness became too much to carry, I hit a wall and realized: *I need to move.* So, I began slowly, gently, and with a new kind of intention. This time, it wasn't about fitness or health goals. It was about creating safety in my own skin, about giving my body permission to release what it had been holding for far too long.

An invitation to attend a restorative yoga class changed everything. I had tried yoga before, but it never stuck. The stillness made me restless. But this time, I walked in with no expectations, just a quiet hope to feel something again. That class brought a kind of relief I hadn't felt in years. The calm, slow pace and the intentional breathwork met me exactly where I was. As I moved through the poses, I accessed layers of tightness I didn't even know I was holding, especially in my hips, where years of stress and emotions had quietly accumulated.

Each breath, each stretch, each pause softened something inside me. My body wasn't just moving; it was listening. This was nervous system regulation. Emotional release. Learning to feel safe in my own skin again. Over time, I explored different kinds of movement that helped me feel grounded: slower, restorative practices when I needed to feel held and safe, stronger movement when I needed to discharge built-up energy, dancing or somatic movement to reconnect with joy and freedom, moving in water, letting the weightlessness help me release tension, and stretching for relief and expansion while focusing on breath to ground myself. The beauty of this deeper physical care is that it's not about the specific activity; it's about cultivating a relationship with your body where you feel safe to release what you've been holding and to ground yourself when everything feels chaotic.

Emotional Care: Releasing What You Have Been Holding Inside

As my body began to feel safer, another layer surfaced—one I had long avoided. Beneath the physical tension lived unspoken emotions that had been waiting patiently to be felt and released. For years, I told myself I was fine. I stayed busy, focused on what needed to get done, moving through my days in a blur of responsibility. Slowing down felt dangerous. It would require me to feel what had been brewing inside. Deep down, I had a fear of what it would mean to face it all. But as my body began to soften its grip, the emotions it had been protecting me from could no longer stay buried. There was grief for the future I had imagined. Fear about what lay ahead. Guilt for the moments I wished things were different. Anger at systems that seemed designed to exhaust me. So many emotions I never expected to carry. I needed a safe place to let it all move through me. My intention was not to fix it or make sense of it, but simply to feel it and let it move on out.

Therapy gave me that. More than coping tools, it gave me permission to feel—a space where I could finally speak the words that I'd only ever whispered to myself. A space to cry without apologizing. To feel anger without being told to be grateful instead. To slowly understand my needs, my fears, and my patterns, and eventually, learn how old hurts were spilling into my present roles as a mother, a wife, and ultimately an adult navigating life.

I began asking myself, *What do I truly want to keep carrying, and what am I ready to lay down? How do I want to live? How do I want to feel?* I also started noticing the power of my inner voice. How easily words could keep me in loops of guilt or self-blame without me even realizing it. Thoughts like:

- *You should be doing more.*

- *You didn't handle that well. She was dysregulated. It wasn't her fault, yet you made it about that.*

- *Everything feels so hard. I'm just so tired. Others can't understand what I go through.*

These thoughts didn't make me weak. They simply revealed how much pain I was holding. But they also kept me stuck. Learning to catch them (to pause, breathe, and choose a kinder story) became a turning point in my healing. Each time I did, I found my way back with compassion instead of criticism. Over time, I learned that healing meant letting emotions move through me, not around me. I needed to be witnessed in my full range of feelings by a professional who could guide me through this exploration and, eventually, by myself.

Alongside therapy, journaling became another space for release. At first, it felt raw and exposing, but in time, it became a way to move energy and make sense of what was stirring within me. Through writing, I could let anger pour out, grieve without a timeline, name my fears, and allow gratitude to appear when it was ready. The more I allowed emotions to move through me, the more room I made inside of me for peace, softness, and moments of joy. This kind of emotional care is something I return to again and again. It isn't something you finish or graduate from; it's an ongoing practice.

I've learned that choosing my thoughts, my words, and my perspective is daily work. It's like tending a garden or strengthening a muscle. It takes gentle, consistent effort. Every day, I choose how I want to show up. Do I want to fall back into old stories, or reach for a kinder truth? Do I want to carry guilt, or set it down and pick up grace instead? These aren't one-time decisions. They're small, moment-to-moment choices that shape not just my inner world but the environment I create for everyone around me. When I offer compassion to myself, I can offer it more freely to my children, my partner, my family and friends, and this beautifully imperfect life we're building together.

Spiritual Care: A Way to Be Held and Supported

As I began to let emotions move through me more freely, another need emerged—one that was less about *doing* and more about *being held.* Held in stillness, in spaces that felt calm and larger than me, and where I could feel less alone. The emotional work had shown me how much I had been trying to control and figure out things on my own. But as my heart opened, I realized how deeply I needed to release some of that burden to something greater than myself.

Spiritual connection looks different for everyone. For some, it's organized religion. For others, it's found in nature, meditation, or quiet presence with oneself. For me, it was a blend of all these things. I rooted in my faith while also finding presence in stillness, nature, the kindness of others, and in the moments that made my body, mind, and spirit feel safe. There is no right or wrong way, only what truly nourishes you.

In my hardest moments, I questioned everything I believed. I wrestled with doubt, anger, and even a sense of abandonment by the divine. But I came to see that these spiritual struggles weren't separate from my healing; they were part of it. Through that realization, I began to see that I also needed moments where I was held instead of being the one holding everyone else.

Spiritual care became a gentle return to trust, even when I couldn't see the bigger picture. It wasn't about finding every answer, but remembering I didn't have to carry everything alone. I began to notice how often I reached for control when I was afraid. Through prayer, time in nature, intentional breathing, and gratitude, I learned that surrender didn't mean giving up. It meant allowing myself to be supported.

Small, spiritual practices became anchors: quiet prayer or conversations with something greater, breathing in nature and feeling connected to life itself, lighting a candle as a reminder of warmth and presence, pausing for gratitude, or simply asking for comfort when everything felt heavy. These moments reminded me that my healing could be supported by something beyond what I could see or understand, that I didn't have to navigate everything from my own strength. Spiritual care helped me move from carrying everything alone to feeling held, even in the uncertainty.

Soulful Care: Finding Your Way Back to Yourself

As I learned to feel safer in my body, allowed emotions to move through me, and connected my spirit to something greater, another question quietly arose: *Who am I when I'm not managing everything? What makes me feel alive? What connects me to joy and allows for moments of happiness?* At first, this question felt almost foreign. How could I focus on myself when my child needed so much? But I began to understand that reconnecting with joy wasn't taking away from my child; it was reclaiming my right to feel alive. It wasn't about false positivity, but about finding small moments of relief that reminded me who I truly was. Not just the part that managed and cared for everyone else, but the part that was curious, creative, playful, and joyful.

The guilt didn't disappear overnight. There were times when choosing joy felt selfish, when I questioned whether I deserved happiness while my child struggled, but over time, I noticed something surprising: The more I honored what made me come alive, the more present and patient I became in my caregiving. Joy wasn't competing with my love for my child; it was enhancing it. To help me reconnect with those parts of myself, I began a practice that a coach and friend introduced me to called *heart storming*, a term that instantly resonated. She described it as a practice of turning inward and reflecting on things that could be part of my soulful path. Unlike brainstorming, which comes from the mind, heart storming begins in the heart. It invites you to *feel* your way toward what brings you alive rather than *think* your way through it.

I sat in stillness with my journal, pen wandering across the page, writing about anything that made my heart light up. I explored what I loved and what I was good at, both professionally and personally. Words, songs, ideas, natural wonders, calming spaces, energizing memories, inspiring people, and curiosity-sparking experiences all found their way onto the page. Later, I'd read through these scattered thoughts and begin to see patterns. Connections emerged naturally. Old passions intertwined with new possibilities. These became gentle indicators, showing me where I felt most at peace, what sparked energy, and what I needed more of to reconnect with my own spark. It became a map back to who I was; one marked by curiosity, creativity, and presence.

The real shift came when I began weaving these small discoveries back into daily life. Not in grand gestures or major transformations, but in tiny, intentional moments. I sought out the things my heart storming had revealed: a few minutes with music that moved me, time in nature that restored me, and creative expression that reminded me I was more than my circumstances. These weren't escapes from reality, but lifelines that helped me stay grounded within it. Each small act of reconnection became a quiet reminder: *You still matter; your aliveness is important.*

I remember making what felt like substantial inner progress and being able to finally ask myself, *What calls to me now? What did I love before life became so heavy? Can I bring any of it back, or is something new waiting to be discovered for who I've become?* I didn't try to force answers. I just listened. Slowly, my days grew less gray and began to fill with color again. Joy wasn't just a memory anymore; it was a possibility. Reconnecting with joy and increasing moments of happiness took many forms. Sometimes, it meant moving whenever my body asked to move. Other times, it was nurturing friendships where I could simply *be* myself, not only "a special-needs mom." It was creating family moments where I could be a daughter, sister, niece, or cousin—not just the caregiver version of me. And sometimes, it meant saying yes to new experiences, like joining a book club with other moms, discussing ideas, and exploring stories beyond my daily life.

My soulful discoveries didn't require grand gestures or hours I didn't have. They simply asked for intention and attention to the small things all around me. Dancing in the kitchen by myself or with the kids, catching a sunset, sending a text or a meme to a friend that made me smile, or keeping a small comfort object nearby. These became quiet ways of weaving joy and strength into ordinary moments. Gradually, I learned to say no to what drained me so I could make space for what brought me back to myself. I allowed myself to want things just for me.

Soulful care reminded me that I was more than what I carried. I was a living, evolving person, worthy of joy, creativity, rest, and meaning beyond my caregiving role. And when I honored that truth, everyone in my life benefited from the fuller, more alive version of me that emerged.

WHEN EVERYTHING INTEGRATES

Exploring these four doorways of healing wasn't linear. Some days, my body demanded attention. Other days, my emotions needed tending to. There were moments when I craved spiritual connection, and times when my soul called out for creative expression or simple joy. As I moved between these areas, something powerful happened. They began to weave together, each one supporting the others. When I moved my body through intentional movement, emotions would surface that I could process in therapy. Journaling helped me understand my body's signals, and spiritual practices gave me the courage to explore joy.

This process unfolded over more than two years of intentional work, and it continues still. Some seasons, I focused intensely on one area. In other seasons, I moved gently between them all. There were setbacks. Sometimes, I felt like I was starting over when old patterns resurfaced. But I learned that stepping backward isn't failure; it's part of the cyclical nature of growth and healing.

This integrated care created a different way of being in the world. Instead of just surviving each day, I began inhabiting my life more fully. I gave myself permission to slow down and listen. In those quiet moments, I learned so much about myself and my process. I started showing up for myself, being more present with my children, being more patient with myself, and more open to joy and peace—even in difficult moments. The ripple effects touched every area of my life.

YOUR OWN WAY FORWARD

Some of what I've shared may resonate with you, some may not. That's exactly as it should be. The key is finding what works for your unique journey and honoring your own timing. What matters is recognizing these four areas as places that can help you move toward deeper peace and connection with yourself. Be patient and extend yourself some grace. This work demands deep vulnerability, radical honesty, and the courage to face difficult truths about your journey.

This deeper self-care may not be something you're ready to explore right away, but when the invitation arrives, when you sense that stirring for something more substantial than quick relief, answering it can be a turning point toward greater acceptance of yourself, your child, and the life you're learning to embrace. What starts as self-care gradually becomes a way of living. A method of returning to yourself that you can carry through all of life's seasons. And when you begin to feel more whole within yourself, something shifts. You become more open to receiving help, to genuine connection with others who understand this journey, and even to those who may not fully understand, but can still support you in it. Next, we'll explore how this inner work prepares you for the outer work of building support systems that can sustain you.

READER REFLECTION:
Exploring Your Doorways

As you consider these four doorways to deeper self-care, remember that this isn't about doing more; it's about becoming more attuned to what truly nourishes you and supports who you are and who you are becoming.

- Which doorway feels most distant right now? Which one feels like a good place to begin?

- **Physical Care:** How are you currently tending to your body? What does it need from you right now? What kind of movement would feel nurturing rather than demanding?

- **Emotional Care:** What have you been carrying that you haven't yet named or shared? What might it feel like to create more space for your emotions?

- **Spiritual Care:** How do you connect to something greater than yourself? What helps you feel supported or held when life feels uncertain?

- **Soulful Care:** What makes you feel most alive? List any passions, hobbies, new experiences, or practices that spark curiosity or joy. What parts of you have gone quiet that might be ready to reemerge?

AFFIRMATION

*I honor my readiness to move beyond quick
fixes toward lasting transformation.
My whole self (physical, emotional, spiritual, and
soulful) deserves attention and care. This deeper
work is sacred. I am gently opening myself to it.*

The Power of Support and Community

FROM YOUR INNER WORLD TO OUTER SUPPORT

As you begin to feel more like someone who belongs in their own life again, something new emerges: the recognition that healing extends beyond the boundaries of your inner world. After spending so much time surviving, tending to others, and quietly rebuilding from within, a shift occurs. The pull to carry everything alone begins to loosen. You start to understand that healing isn't solely an inward journey. It also unfolds in relationship, in community, in being truly seen and supported. Authentic self-care includes knowing when to let others in. We aren't designed to navigate this alone. When we reach the place where we can admit, "I need help," we open ourselves to transformation. Vulnerability becomes a bridge. Honesty becomes release. And gradually, the weight begins to lift.

THE MODERN PARENTING CHALLENGE

Parenting can feel incredibly lonely; extended family often lives far away, work and life move at a pace that doesn't slow down, and what used to be common (grandparents living nearby, siblings around the corner, neighbors who know your kids) is harder to come by these days. We're doing so much parenting on our own. And when you're raising a child with special needs, that isolation can feel even heavier. Our children's needs are complex, and not everyone understands what that really means. The combination can be overwhelming. We feel it everywhere: in our bodies, in our relationships, and in how much energy we have left for our children and for ourselves.

This is why finding our people matters so much. Family members who truly get it, friends who show up, babysitters we trust, therapists who understand, respite care that gives us breathing room, and programs that work for our kids. Essentially, we welcome anyone who can help share the load. It's what makes this unique type of parenting sustainable.

THE LIFELINE OF PRACTICAL SUPPORT

Support comes in many forms, but perhaps the most essential is the kind that creates actual space for you to rest and reset. This isn't about emotional validation alone, though that matters deeply. It's about someone actually stepping in so you can step away, breathe, and remember who you are beyond this caregiving role. The demands can be relentless, and the constant need to be "on" can overwhelm even the strongest of us. The relief that comes from someone shouldering the responsibility, even temporarily, is profound. It becomes an essential lifeline not just for our physical health, but for our emotional well-being and our sense of connection to the larger world.

These pockets of time allow you to:

- Rest and have some "me" time

- Recharge your depleted energy

- Remember who you are beyond caregiving

- Approach challenges from a centered place rather than exhaustion

- Sustain the pace that this journey often demands

- Feel less alone in carrying such a complex load

Respite care isn't a luxury; it's a necessity. Whether it's through formal programs, trusted family members, or volunteers who understand the unique needs of your child, these moments are everything. Other forms of practical relief might include:

- Childcare so you can rest, run errands, or simply sit in quiet

- Help with household tasks, meals, or transportation

- Guidance navigating IEPs, therapies, or medical systems

- Volunteer "buddy" programs through local organizations that pair families with trained helpers

The beauty of practical help is immediate: The overwhelm lessens, your breathing deepens, and you remember that you don't have to hold it all alone. Even a few hours can replenish you enough to show up for your child and yourself with renewed presence and peace.

COMMUNITY OFFERINGS

Emotional Healing: Your emotional well-being matters. Find spaces where you can share openly and be met with empathy, not judgment. Be validated by others who truly understand. Experience both laughter and tears without apology. Medical professionals, therapists, coaches, healing circles, support groups, and spiritual/religious mentors can offer you the emotional space you deserve.

A Sense of Belonging: When others don't fully understand your world, feelings of isolation can grow. But inside the right community, you don't have to explain everything in order to be seen. Your small wins are celebrated with big hearts. You're reminded again and again that you are not alone. Belonging provides comfort, but it's also essential for the heart.

Hope and Perspective: Support doesn't just help you survive; it helps you see what's still possible. You witness others who have walked similar roads with courage, their resilience becoming a quiet roadmap for your own journey. You hear stories that mirror your own struggles and others that expand your understanding of what's possible. Hope is contagious within a community, and sometimes, hearing someone else say "me too" is the most healing thing of all.

Digital and Virtual Connection: There are times when the right support isn't in your immediate environment. Online communities, virtual support groups, and social media connections can offer profound understanding and practical wisdom. This is especially true if your local area lacks specific resources, your schedule makes in-person meetings impossible, you need support in the wee hours of the night when you can't sleep, or you're seeking connection with parents facing a similar *Thing*. The screen doesn't diminish the realness of the connection. Deep friendships can be found through online groups. These are the people who can be by your side during this journey, checking in during tough weeks, celebrating small victories, and understanding without explanation.

FINDING MY FIRST SAFE SPACE

As I explored my inner landscape, a need to tend to my outer world began to emerge. In order to feel less alone, I had to take a step outward. That truth led me to seek a place where I could slow down enough to be honest about what I was carrying and where that honesty would be welcome. The opportunity for a meditation class found me through social media. I wasn't sure what to expect, but a friend agreed to go with me, and later that night, we found ourselves in a beautiful studio with a skilled facilitator. In time, she would become a dear friend and an important guide on my journey. It was a new and gentle space that felt both welcoming and safe.

Her studio offered more than mindfulness classes; it was a sanctuary, a place of calm, nervous system relief, and quiet honesty where I sat alongside others who were also weary, also seeking. We weren't there to fix ourselves. We were there to rest, to breathe, to simply *be*. This wasn't therapy or a specialized support group. It was a gathering of people choosing to slow down in a space where vulnerability felt safe. Each person arrived carrying different life experiences, and that diversity created safety. I could explore healing without immediately naming or claiming specific challenges.

The practices she offered gently reconnected me with parts of myself I hadn't touched in years. I had been so focused on holding everything together that I hadn't noticed how far I'd drifted from real connection, the kind that doesn't add pressure or weight, just presence and realness. By feeling safe around others and hearing their struggles, I began to feel safer being honest about my own. I found community and understanding in this space and, in time, grew more comfortable sharing my truth and my vulnerabilities. That safe space prepared me for a different kind of connection, one I had been contemplating for a while, but hadn't felt ready for until I had strengthened my voice and resilience first.

THE EMBRACE I DIDN'T KNOW I NEEDED

As I continued to reconnect with myself through various safe spaces and practices, I noticed another shift: I no longer acted from a place of desperation, but from grounded clarity. I wasn't waiting to be saved or understood. I was learning to speak with honesty and advocate for my needs with newfound courage. That inner clarity eventually led me to a step I had been quietly circling: joining a special-needs moms' group. This felt different, bigger, more exposing. It wasn't just about finding community; it was about facing the journey head-on. I was learning to meet it with openness, grace, and a deeper kind of strength. I was also seeking a different kind of understanding, the kind that comes from shared experience.

I remember feeling nervous on my way there, with so many emotions swirling inside me. But when I walked into that space, my whole body released. From my head to my toes, it was like a balloon deflating, a deep breath I hadn't realized I was holding. This space felt different. It was like a big hug I didn't know I needed. We shared stories, resources, and hard-won wisdom. But more than anything, we shared *truth*. There was no pretending. Just women showing up as they were: honest, vulnerable, and resilient.

Some stories were heavy, met with silent understanding and knowing nods. Other times, we laughed at the absurd moments only we could fully appreciate: the public meltdowns and the unexpected things our children said or did. That kind of shared truth is its own medicine. There's something powerful about being truly understood. When you're surrounded by others who've walked similar paths, there's an unspoken understanding that cuts through isolation. They see you as a whole person, deserving of care and connection. In this space, I realized the deeper importance of community, not only for the resources and practical help, but for the profound connection that allows us to heal. We don't just need tools for our children; we need spaces for ourselves. Spaces where we can be truly held and supported.

LEARNING TO RECEIVE

As I softened into greater self-awareness, something fundamental shifted within me. I became more willing to ask for help and, more importantly, to receive help. The old narratives (*I have to do it all. No one will understand. I'll be a burden.*) began to loosen their grip. The truth is, support had been available to me all along. My family and friends had always offered love. But in some seasons, I wasn't in the right place to receive it. I was too tangled in guilt, fear, and the pressure to be the "strong one." As I grew into this new chapter, I began to recognize love for what it truly was: steady, generous, and patiently waiting for me to be ready.

Letting that love in changed everything. Feeling supported gave me the courage to say yes to invitations I once would have declined: reconnecting with old friends, exploring creative outlets, and opening myself to new experiences. I began to notice those around me with new eyes: the kindness in strangers and the quiet ways people show they care. Every gesture, big or small, became a reminder that I wasn't alone. These offerings of support reignited my tired heart. It's this softening process that allows us to belong. It's how we remember that we were never meant to do this alone.

THE PEOPLE WHO REALLY SEE YOUR CHILD

There's another layer of support that deserves recognition: the therapists, teachers, and professionals who devote their lives to caring for our children and helping them reach their potential. These are the people who look past *The Thing* and can often see our child more easily than we can. They celebrate our child's smallest victories as if they were their own. They never give up, even when progress feels slow. They become more than service providers; they become part of your extended family, your village, your hope. The speech therapist who finally finds the approach that unlocks your child's communication. The occupational therapist who makes therapy feel like play. The teacher who creates a classroom where your child feels safe to be themselves. When you find these people, treasure them. Thank them often. They are choosing to make your child's life (and your life) better every single day.

And then there are the unexpected moments of grace: strangers who see you and your child and restore your sense of hope and love in the world, even if just for a moment. The cashier who patiently waits while your child carefully tries to ring up their own items. The other parent at the playground who genuinely engages with your child instead of looking away. The stranger who sees your child's meltdown and offers understanding instead of annoyance. These moments matter more than these strangers will ever know. In a world that can feel harsh and unwelcoming, their simple kindness reminds you that there is still good. That your child's presence in the world can inspire connection and compassion.

THE CHOICE TO CONNECT

Support is essential. Asking for help doesn't make you weak; it makes you human. It's an act of courage, self-trust, and opening your heart to the truth that you were never meant to carry this burden alone. When someone takes the weight from your shoulders, even briefly, something profound happens. You remember what it feels like to breathe fully. To think clearly. To move through your day from a place of centeredness rather than survival. This shared connection is what makes the long journey sustainable. And as you allow others in, you discover something even more powerful: You're not the only one walking this path. Your child's journey, in all its complexity, is full of meaning. Your story is worthy of being held with tenderness, too.

Your people, the ones who truly see you, are out there, waiting with open arms. Seek them out. Welcome them. Allow this journey to become a little lighter. Because once we feel held by others, we begin to hold ourselves differently, too. From that place of connection and steadiness, we can move toward something essential: greater acceptance of ourselves, our children, and this complex journey we're navigating together.

READER REFLECTION:
Strengthening Your Support Network

- **Assess Your Support:** Who do you turn to right now? Make a list of the people, groups, or professionals who support you emotionally, practically, or through guidance and information.

- **Name What's Missing:** What kind of support do you need more of? Emotional encouragement, practical help, connection, or understanding?

- **Take One Step:** What could help strengthen your support system? Could you join a group, reach out to a friend, or seek professional help?

- **Notice Your Barriers:** How do you feel when asking for help? Do you hold back? What fears or stories come up when you do?

- **Give Back When You Can:** How might you offer support to others? A kind word, a text, a shared resource? Small gestures often mean the most.

AFFIRMATION

I don't have to do this by myself.
It is safe to lean on others, to share my truth,
and to allow myself to be supported.

Inching Toward Acceptance

WHEN SOMETHING SHIFTS

Imagine you're in your kitchen making coffee when you notice your shoulders have dropped. You're not tense, braced for what's coming. You're just standing there, watching the water heat up —not running through your to-do list. Not mentally preparing for what could go wrong. You are simply present with your coffee, your body relaxed in a way it hasn't been in months, maybe years. It's such a small moment. But for so long, every quiet space has been filled with *The Thing*: constant mental noise, overwhelming worry replaying over and over, and searching for solutions you don't have. The weight that has made simple tasks exhausting because half your energy was always somewhere else. But right now, you're just making coffee, your body remembering what ease feels like.

This is what acceptance (or something like it) actually looks like. Not some big moment of surrender, but finding small spaces where your mind gets to rest. Where you're not fighting your reality or trying to fix it. Just moving through your morning like someone who belongs in their own life again. Some call this acceptance. Others call it settling in, surrender, or finding ease with what is. The name matters less than noticing when it shows up. And for me, it started showing up in moments I had been missing for so long, the ones where I hadn't been fully present because my mind was always somewhere else.

WHEN I LOST MYSELF

For years, I threw myself into helping my daughter "catch up." She never asked me to, but this was simply the version of love I knew how to offer when everything felt unfamiliar and overwhelming. She tried it all because I put so many things in front of her—therapies, intensives, and programs that promised "progress." If someone mentioned a possibility, I was already filling out paperwork.

It came from a place of love, yes, but underneath that love lived something else: fear of a future that was uncertain, quiet grief for the motherhood I'd imagined, and a persistent feeling that if I wasn't constantly doing something, then I was failing her. I became consumed by the need for action. Our days revolved around appointments and assessments, goals and benchmarks. For her, it meant a childhood filtered through the lens of progress. For me, it meant running on empty from decision fatigue that left me hollow by evening.

When our son was born, the weight doubled. I convinced myself that burnout was just part of motherhood, that self-sacrifice meant love, that needing rest was weakness. The breaking point didn't come dramatically; it came quietly: the morning I struggled to get out of bed, the medical follow-up I kept rescheduling, the evening I sat in my car in the driveway, too depleted to walk inside. And then, somewhere in the blur of it all, I had to stop because I finally recognized that my children needed me to slow down. More importantly, I needed me to slow down.

THE REAL SHIFT

For a long time, I feared that if I stopped trying to fix everything, I'd be giving up on my daughter. I was afraid that finding peace with our reality meant settling for less. I worried that it meant I didn't love her enough to keep fighting. But now, I can finally see that my child was never broken. There was never anything to fix. And if I'm honest, my deepest shift came when I stopped pretending my dedication was noble. It wasn't about protecting her or advocating for what she deserved. It was about me and my fear of failing her, my desperate grip on the story I'd written before I even knew who she was.

Real peace isn't passive resignation. It's actively choosing to meet reality with openness rather than constant resistance. It's the difference between "this shouldn't be happening" and "this is happening." This shift began when I stopped measuring her worth by milestones and truly saw her for who she is: a child who loves deeply, laughs freely, and finds wonder in the smallest things.

This is a complex theme to explore because it looks different for each parent. It's not about right or wrong, better or worse. Each journey is simply unique. Some find a deep sense of acceptance and calling in their journey, a genuine feeling that this path was meant for them. Others settle into something quieter, a growing peace with what is, moments where they can simply be with their reality without fighting it. And some genuinely struggle to find peace at all. They may move through the days doing what needs to be done, but the acceptance (the ease) remains out of reach. The weight stays heavy, and that's real, too. All of these experiences are valid.

WHAT BECOMES POSSIBLE

Finding some measure of peace with our reality didn't make the hard days disappear, but it changed how I carried them. There are still moments of frustration, days when sadness settles in, times when I feel overwhelmed or uncertain and afraid. But now, there's more space between the trigger and the overwhelm. More moments when my thoughts aren't as clouded by hard emotions, leaving room for more of the lighter ones to surface. In practical terms, this looks like:

- Focusing on the things that did go well in an outing rather than only what didn't

- Choosing activities based on what brings joy rather than what builds skills

- Finding rhythm in the extra time it takes to do simple things

- Understanding that some days will be harder than others without a clear reason why

- Saying no to therapies that drain more than they give

- Learning that "okay" doesn't mean perfect; it means real, present, and enough

- Understanding that not everyone will get it, and that's okay

Part of this shift meant learning to work with my child's reality rather than against it. Instead of expecting her to be calm in overstimulating environments, I began anticipating that she might struggle at times. This allowed me to prepare her beforehand, plan for breaks, or redirect her attention when needed. When I started making these adjustments, something unexpected happened: The moments when things went better than expected felt like genuine victories rather than simply avoided disappointments.

This approach also meant advocating for her needs by speaking up when she required something—or when those around us, whether family or friends, could make small accommodations to reduce her overwhelm. Having learned to recognize her typical reaction patterns in certain situations, I could anticipate challenges and proactively request adjustments that would help her succeed. This meant, sometimes, asking people to give her a few minutes to ease into being in a new place when she felt overwhelmed by lots of people. Giving her time to come to them when she was ready, instead of expecting that she needed to immediately go to them and say hi or jump into an activity at a birthday party or outing.

As I began to feel more grounded in our reality, the emotional cloud that had been hovering over everything started to lift. I found myself more present, choosing to see the good instead of just the hard and the different. My moments were calmer, less full of worry or a need for control. I started caring more about what I thought and less about what others thought. I started feeling braver, more confident in who I was and who we were as a family. I could move through situations more easily. I felt lighter, like a gentle wind that bends around obstacles instead of fighting them. This meant finding my way through with less force and struggle.

I also felt more comfortable being vulnerable and honest in conversations about my family, but mainly about myself. And in that openness, I often discovered other people's vulnerabilities or struggles that helped me realize we all have stuff. We just don't talk about it openly most of the time. The isolation that came from feeling like my family was the only one going through something difficult began to lift when I stopped hiding and started sharing. Where I once felt heavy and resistant, I now moved with something closer to grace. Not perfect, but there were these moments where I could feel myself flowing instead of pushing, accepting instead of fighting, and trusting instead of controlling.

WHEN THE HARD QUESTIONS STILL COME

Even in this newly found space you might be visiting more often, certain hard questions may still arise: "Why us? Why this path?" These questions come quietly, in the tired moments, when you're watching other families and wondering about the road not taken. And when these questions darken your mind, the emotions (especially guilt for daring to think or say something like that) hit you like a ton of bricks.

When I brought this up with my therapist, she offered something to consider: What if, over time, I could work toward shifting the question from, "Why me?" to "Why not me?" She was clear that this wasn't a perspective that would come easily, but suggested it as something to gently move toward. Asking, "Why not us to hold this particular kind of love?" changed my perspective. The guilt begins to lift when you realize that wondering doesn't make you a bad parent or an ungrateful person. It makes you human. You can love your child deeply and still feel the weight of this unexpected journey.

I won't pretend this perspective shift happens easily or stays put. Sometimes, the only honest response is, "I don't know why, but I'm here. We're here. And that's enough for today." But in the gentlest moments, when you see your child's pure joy or witness their unique way of moving through the world, the question might quietly transform. Perhaps, we were meant to walk the road that would expand our hearts in ways we never imagined.

THE JOURNEY BACK AND FORTH

You find some peace, settle into it a little more, and then life happens. Maybe you're tired (really tired), and your patience is paper thin when your child has a meltdown in the grocery store, or struggles to sit still during dinner, or jumps from activity to activity without finishing anything. Acceptance can also escape when your child has a bathroom accident when they're well past the age where that is supposed to happen, or has an unsettling interaction with another child at the park. In those moments, when you're running on empty, and your child needs more than you feel capable of giving, all that hard-won peace can feel out of reach.

It's in these depleted moments that the comparison trap opens widest. You see other families moving through their day with what looks like such ease, and the old questions resurface: "Why can't this just be simpler? Why does everything have to be so hard?" Sometimes, it's triggered by something specific: a behavior that pushes every button you have, a reaction you can't understand no matter how hard you try, or the accumulation of small challenges that leaves you feeling overwhelmed and reactive. You might snap more easily, feel that familiar frustration rising, or find yourself grieving all over again for the easier path you thought you'd be walking. Suddenly, you find yourself pulled back into resistance, into that old familiar fight against what is. That's okay. Peace (or acceptance) isn't a destination you reach once and stay at forever. It's a place you visit, leave, and return to. Maybe it means learning that you don't need to choose between the gratitude and the pain. Maybe it's sitting with it all, giving yourself a little time to let the feelings move through you, and finding your center again.

The gift isn't staying there forever. Instead, it's learning the way home. Each time you find your way back, the path becomes clearer, the journey shorter. You don't dwell as long on the hurt or even the anger at yourself if you were reactive or overwhelmed. You simply feel it and then remember the way back and what it feels like—that ability to breathe more freely and lighter, to see clearly, to replace those feelings of your own anger or frustration with feelings of love and compassion for your struggling child. You carry that wisdom with you, even in the difficult moments. You begin to trust that even when you're overwhelmed again, even when the old feelings resurface, that quiet knowing persists. That softness remains, waiting for you to return to it again and again.

WHERE IT LEADS

When that shift happens, you begin to notice what was always there: your child's genuine affection, a word or gesture after months of waiting, a quiet moment of connection that means everything. One day, you realize you've learned to trust that you can handle whatever comes. You find yourself speaking up more naturally, advocating not just for your child but for this life you've built together. If you're still figuring it out, still in the thick of it, that's okay. Your feelings don't make you weak. Your struggles don't make you a bad parent. Your humanity doesn't disqualify you from this work of loving a child who needs extra support.

This kind of peace comes quietly, gradually, and sometimes when you least expect it. And when it arrives, it won't feel like an ending.

It will feel like a return to breath, to ease, to yourself. You're showing up. You're growing, day by day, one gentle return at a time. And in this return to yourself, something else begins to stir. The heart that has learned to hold its own struggle with tenderness starts to sense another possibility: greater forgiveness for yourself and others who have crossed your path on this journey.

READER REFLECTION:
Your Journey Toward Acceptance

Acceptance isn't a finish line but a path we keep walking. Some days, we move forward with ease. Other days, our steps feel heavy and uncertain. There's no right way to do this, no timeline you're supposed to follow. Gently ask yourself:

- **Where are you today?** Are you beginning to find small moments of peace? Notice where you are without judgment.

- **What does acceptance feel like for you?** Maybe it's a moment when your shoulders drop, when you stop fighting what is, or when you catch yourself simply being present.

- **How has your perspective shifted?** Do things that once felt impossible now feel softer? Have your definitions of "progress" or "okay" started to change?

- **What does acceptance look like in your daily life?** Is it celebrating small wins instead of focusing on what went wrong? Choosing rest or joy over constant doing? Saying no to things that drain you?

- **How do you find your way back?** When you slip into resistance or grief, what helps you return? A deep breath, a moment of stillness, some space to yourself, or remembering what you're grateful for?

When you next feel overwhelmed, pause and choose one small action. This can be a slow breath, a short walk, or simply placing a hand on your heart. Practice it once this week. Notice how it feels to move through the moment instead of fighting it.

AFFIRMATION

I can meet life as it is, even when it's difficult.
Acceptance isn't something I achieve; it's something I practice.
My child and I are enough in this moment, exactly as we are.

CHAPTER 10

Forgiveness and Letting Go

THE QUIET WEIGHT AFTER ACCEPTANCE

There's a whisper that follows acceptance. Something that moves through the quiet spaces as we practice making peace with what is. In that stillness, forgiveness begins its slow, almost hidden work. Even after we stop resisting our reality and begin to soften into it, a heaviness can remain. Much of that weight is guilt. Guilt over what we think we did wrong, what we didn't see coming, or what we couldn't prevent.

We all have moments we wish we could do over, days when we feel overwhelmed, and times where we snap at people we love or simply fall short of our own expectations. I used to believe I had to carry all these moments with me as proof of my failures, but there's another layer, too: guilt over the moments when we rejected ourselves, our children, or the people we love most. Acceptance helps us find peace with what is, but forgiveness helps us release what was. It's learning to separate guilt that serves our growth from guilt that simply punishes us for being human.

UNLOADING THE BACKPACK

No one prepares you for the emotional weight of this path. It builds slowly, layer by layer, tucked between therapies, long days, and the pressure to hold everything together. Often, it's hidden behind the smile you wear for your child, your family, and the world. That quiet weight makes you feel like you are carrying a heavy backpack everywhere you go. Inside that backpack are all the "what ifs," "should haves," and the guilt and blame you carry for things that were never really your fault. Guilt showed up as a familiar companion on this path, creating a quiet, constant inventory:

- "What if I caused this? What if I missed the warning signs?"

- "I should have been more patient. I should have handled that better."

- "I'm being selfish for wanting time to myself."

- "Other parents seem to handle being a special-needs parent so much better than I do."

- "I shouldn't feel sad about our new reality. I should be grateful."

- "Am I doing enough? Did I miss something?"

- "I turned away when they needed me most."

- "I rejected help when people offered because I thought I should handle it alone."

These questions didn't just live in my head; they settled in my body—in the tension in my shoulders, in the tightness in my chest, and in the heaviness that built up over months. The hardest part? The guilt around moments when I felt like I had turned away from the people I love most. Times when I pulled back from my child because their emotions felt too big for me to handle. Moments when I pushed my spouse away because I was drowning and couldn't admit I needed help. Days when I was so hard on myself that I forgot I deserved kindness, too. What I needed wasn't more strategy or strength. What I needed was to be gentle with myself and offer myself forgiveness for the moments I couldn't be who I wanted to be.

PRACTICING SELF-COMPASSION

There was a point in my journey when I noticed I was offering grace to everyone but myself. In most moments, I showed up with patience for my child and understanding for my friends, but inside, I allowed a harsh inner voice to judge me and hold me to impossible standards. During a therapy session, my therapist helped me realize how hard I was on myself. She asked me, "What would happen if you looked at yourself the way you look at other mothers you care about? What would you see then?"

She invited me into a simple exercise: "Think of a moment where you were struggling as a mother. Now, imagine watching it from the outside. That woman you see is you. What would you say to her?" I thought of a meltdown at the park that had happened just a few days prior. My daughter was overwhelmed, I was exhausted, and the afternoon was unraveling fast. I felt defeated. Embarrassed. Alone in the chaos. In that moment, my patience wore thin, and I didn't act in the best way I could. I realized that guilt was still present, attacking my well-being.

But when I imagined watching that moment from the outside (not as me, but as a mother who knew how hard parenting is), I didn't see failure. I saw someone doing her best. Someone tired, tender, and giving everything she had. I didn't want to criticize her. I wanted to comfort her. This became my first real glimpse of what forgiveness could look like. Not excusing what happened, but seeing it through eyes of compassion rather than judgment.

MY BACKPACK

For me, forgiveness became the process of slowly unpacking a heavy backpack I had been carrying for years, gently removing each item and carefully setting it down. It meant observing and examining every weight I had held, understanding why I carried it, and ultimately, allowing myself to leave it behind. Once I started unpacking, I discovered that I could feel so much stronger and freer without all that extra weight. I could learn from my mistakes without punishing myself for them.

Forgiveness wasn't saying my feelings didn't matter. It was recognizing that carrying them around was exhausting me, and I deserved to travel lighter. Over time, I began to notice when guilt was taking over. It felt like a tightness in my chest, a knot forming in my stomach, that harsh inner voice taking over my thoughts. Each time I forgave myself, I felt a little lighter. Not because everything was fixed, but because I was finally letting myself be human. I also had to learn to leave the past in the past. I couldn't change what had already happened, and reliving those moments or carrying that weight into my present was unnecessary and making my journey heavier. Here's what I came to understand: I made choices with the information, the capacity, and the heart I had at the time. I showed up again and again and did everything I could with what I had.

WHEN FORGIVENESS FEELS DIFFICULT

For a long time, guilt felt safer than forgiveness. If I felt bad about the past, I didn't have to risk making new mistakes. Guilt became familiar—uncomfortable, but known. Forgiveness asked me to be kind to myself, which felt scarier than the guilt and negative voice I was used to. I initially resisted because I thought forgiveness meant giving up accountability. I worried that if I stopped feeling guilty, then I'd be letting myself off the hook. But I learned that forgiveness isn't about lowering my standards; it's about releasing guilt that was keeping me from joy.

Some wounds need time to heal before they can be forgiven. Some hurts need to be fully felt before they can be released. I learned to give myself permission to be exactly where I was in this process. On the days when I couldn't forgive, I tried this exercise instead:

- Simply notice the pain without trying to fix it.

- Hold space for my anger and disappointment.

- Remember that resistance is part of the process, too.

- Trust that when I'm ready, forgiveness will be there, waiting.

LETTERS TO MYSELF: A PATH TO HEALING

Eventually, my therapist gently suggested another tool for forgiveness: "What if you wrote letters of forgiveness to yourself?" At first, I was confused and felt a wave of resistance. *Forgive myself? What would that sound like? More importantly, how would it feel?* She explained it wasn't just one letter; it would require writing various letters—one to each version of myself that I needed to forgive:

- The younger me, still carrying old wounds.

- The new mother, terrified and overwhelmed.

- The fierce advocate, tired but unwavering.

- The devoted parent, giving so much, but still feeling it wasn't enough.

- The wife who felt overwhelmed in her marriage.

- The person who had been so hard on herself for so long.

Each letter became a quiet act of liberation, a way to honor what I had carried, before gently laying it down. Forgiveness didn't erase the past, but it did change my relationship to it. It gave me room to breathe again. These letters were challenging, and it took a few months from when she suggested it to when I felt ready to sit down and write them. Part of this resistance came from the fear of letting go of something that, even though not helpful, had been a familiar companion.

LEARNING TO TRAVEL LIGHTER

Forgiveness isn't a single moment of release. It's a gentle, ongoing practice of choosing compassion over criticism, understanding over judgment, and peace over the weight of what was. I'm learning to speak to myself the way I would speak to someone I deeply love who is struggling. The voice within me had been speaking harshly for far too long. It held me to impossible standards, replayed my mistakes, and convinced me I had to carry guilt that was never mine to hold. But that voice can learn a new language—one of tenderness and grace.

I am not the sum of my difficult moments. I am not defined by the days I felt overwhelmed or the times I wished I had handled things differently. I am a whole person: beautifully imperfect, deeply loving, and worthy of the same compassion I so freely give to others. I'm learning to choose what goes into my backpack now. Instead of guilt, sadness, and anger taking up all the space, I'm making room for joy and compassion for myself and those around me.

And as I travel lighter, I can lift my head and notice what's around me. I can be more present for the small moments that make up our days. When you're not constantly looking backward with regret or bracing for what's ahead, something shifts. You start to see what's right in front of you. The ordinary beauty you've been missing—this is where presence lives. Not in the big moments we plan for, but in the small ones we almost overlook. And it's in that presence that joy quietly finds its way back in.

READER REFLECTION:
Your Forgiveness Journey

- Where have I been holding myself to impossible standards, and what would it look like to meet myself with the same compassion I offer others?

- Which parts or past versions of myself are asking for forgiveness? What might be freed when I finally release that weight?

- Who still holds space in my heart that I'm ready to forgive so I can reclaim my peace (whether connected to this journey or not)?

- When forgiveness feels hard, what fears or beliefs make it difficult to soften? How can I simply hold space for where I am today?

- What guilt, shame, or sadness am I ready to set down? What lighter emotions (like love, grace, or joy) do I want to carry instead?

AFFIRMATION

I am setting down the weight I've been carrying.
I forgive myself for being human and release
the guilt that's been holding me back.
I choose to travel lighter.

Finding Presence and Joy in the Journey

THE PROMISE OF WHAT'S ALREADY HERE

used to think joy would come when things got easier—when we had fewer appointments, when milestones came more naturally, when life felt less overwhelming. But somewhere along this journey, I began to wonder, *What if I am looking in the wrong places?* Joy isn't found somewhere in the future. It isn't to be put on hold while you're waiting for your life to change. It's woven into the moments you're living right now, hidden within your current reality. But to find it, you first have to be able to lift your head and notice what's around you.

When you learn to travel lighter, to set down some of the guilt and soften the harsh voice within, something new becomes possible. You can be more present in your life as it is right now. Not the life you wish you had or living in fear of what it might become, but being present in the life that actually is. This kind of presence has become distant and foreign in our achievement-oriented world. It requires something we rarely give ourselves permission for: the ability to slow down and just be. To gradually shift our focus from what isn't to what is.

BREAKING FREE FROM SURVIVAL MODE

In survival mode, everything feels urgent. You're always bracing for the next challenge. Your mind loops endlessly through worry and what-ifs, never quite settling into the present moment. There's an exhausting pressure to always be doing something: planning the next therapy session, researching interventions, preparing for potential meltdowns, and staying three steps ahead of every possible scenario. You pour so much energy into worrying about outcomes you can't predict, trying to control scenarios that may never happen. You convince yourself that rest must be earned, but the lists never end, and the doing never stops. Somewhere in the constant motion, you lose yourself entirely.

When you honor your need for restoration, even occasionally, you can hold space for your child's big emotions without losing yourself in them. When you're mindful of refilling your reserves, presence becomes more accessible. Rest also creates space for new ideas to emerge, for reevaluating existing approaches, and for seeing future possibilities that weren't visible in the constant motion of survival mode.

A MOMENT THAT CHANGED EVERYTHING

Sometimes, our children become our greatest teachers without even trying. For me, an important lesson came during a routine car ride home with my daughter. As we neared our house, I caught a glimpse of her in my side mirror. There she was, head slightly out the window, hair flowing in the wind, waving at neighbors, and calling out to animals she spotted along the way. Pure joy radiated from her face as she soaked in every detail of our familiar street.

She was completely present, and I was not. While she was lost in the simple pleasure of the wind on her face, my mind was tangled in the long to-do list waiting for me at home. But it wasn't just her presence that struck me. It was how she noticed everything I was rushing past. The neighbors I barely acknowledged. The animals I didn't see. The trees and details of our street that I drive by every day, but rarely notice or appreciate.

In contrast to her joy and awareness, versus my preoccupation, something stirred inside of me. I realized how much life I was missing, trapped in thoughts that didn't belong in the present moment I was sharing with her. In fact, I had disconnected myself from her, from her joy, from her awareness. That moment invited me back to her, yes, but it also invited me back to myself. I deserved to live the life I was protecting, not just survive it. And living requires the courage to stop constantly doing and planning, and instead, simply be. After that rearview mirror moment, I made a quiet promise to myself: I would stop to feel the sun on my skin, to hear my kids' laughter, to let moments be meaningful instead of just productive. To rest, not as a reward for completing everything, but as a way of honoring myself and my right to rest.

WHEN PRESENCE BECOMES AVAILABLE

I learned to see presence as an invitation to slow down and enjoy what is happening in the present moment. Presence doesn't erase the challenges or eliminate the planning your family relies on, but it changes how you carry it all. Instead of being swept away by the endless mental loop of past regrets and future worries, presence invites you to pause, soften into now, and remember that your ability to be with what is allows both you and your child to feel safe and steady. Now, presence shows up in my everyday moments:

- In the middle of a meltdown, when I pause instead of immediately reacting

- When I stay soft during transitions, even when every instinct wants to brace

- When I choose calm, not because I feel it naturally but because I want to create that experience for myself and my family

- When I offer myself grace after a difficult day instead of harsh judgment

- When I choose presence over productivity, simply being over doing

- When I allow myself to rest when I need it

- When I say no to a therapy session and choose rest or unstructured time with my family instead

These small acts of presence gradually build into something larger. They lead to a fundamental shift in how you approach your days.

BUILDING YOUR OWN REGULATION TOOLS

I learned that presence isn't just about intention. When you're triggered by your child's big emotions, when your body is flooded with frustration or overwhelm, good intentions aren't enough. You need something to anchor you back to the present moment, something that helps you pause before you react. This realization led me to start experimenting with different approaches to staying calm and present. As I grew more consistent and aware of my self-care needs, these regulation tools became more accessible.

I discovered that my ability to regulate my emotions came through increased "me" time, quiet spaces, and creative outlets. My partner discovered he needed active movement and working with his hands to release and process stress. My daughter responded to music, dance, and movement when she felt overwhelmed. My son benefited from activities that required calm and focus, including building Legos or coloring.

Having these options available and accessible helped create increased spaces of pause before big reactions. As a parent, they helped me recognize familiar stress patterns before they took over. I started unlearning reactive habits, noticing the constant no's I unconsciously repeated throughout the day, often coming from my own lack of patience and awareness rather than what the moment actually needed. This awareness helped me develop skills that were beneficial to myself and my family. These small shifts began to counter the relentless societal pressure to always be productive.

Instead of measuring my worth through constant output, I began valuing presence and connection. I was more in tune with creating spaces for each individual and us as a family unit to have tools when stress was growing: taking a few deep breaths (or "balloon breaths") together before difficult transitions, creating quiet retreat spaces, and establishing rhythms that honored everyone's different sensory and regulation needs. All of this led to an overwhelming truth. I'm not just building these practices for ordinary days. I'm building them for the moments when the ground shifts beneath me.

WHEN THESE SKILLS BECOME A LIFELINE

As a special-needs parent, this can show up when you receive an additional diagnosis that reshapes everything you thought you knew about your child's future: a triggering medical situation where your body wants to shut down but you need to stay present, a harsh comment from a stranger in public who doesn't understand why your child is melting down, and suddenly you're fighting shame even though you know better, or the teacher who dismisses your concerns, who speaks about your child with frustration right in front of you—someone who should be caring for them but is treating them as an inconvenience, and the betrayal cuts deeper because you trusted them.

These are the moments when everything you've been practicing becomes essential. When you can pause, even for three breaths, before responding to news that devastates you. When you can ground yourself enough to actually hear what the doctor is saying instead of drowning in panic. When you can let that stranger's judgment roll past you because you're anchored in what you know about your child and yourself. When you can walk into that meeting, heart pounding, and still speak clearly about what your child needs instead of reacting from your most wounded place.

Presence doesn't make these moments hurt less. You still feel the grief, the fear, and the disappointment, but it creates space between the event and your response, between the pain and the spiral. It lets you feel your emotions without being consumed by them or fracturing. And perhaps, most importantly, these tools help you return to yourself afterward. Instead of staying stuck in the trauma of that diagnosis, that comment, or that betrayal, you can process what happened, release what you need to release, and slowly come back to your center. You remember that one hard moment doesn't define your entire journey. That you can hold space for the difficulty while still accessing the strength you've built, the love that grounds you, and the resilience that keeps showing up even when everything feels impossible. This is where all the small daily practices reveal their true purpose. They're preparing you for when you need them most.

FROM SURVIVAL TO SUSTAINABLE RHYTHM

With these tools and this growing awareness, something began to shift in me. I started moving from constant survival mode into a more sustainable rhythm, learning to flow between challenge and ease, effort and rest, holding on and letting go. I used to think thriving was a constant state of ease and something very out of reach, but I have learned it is not a destination or a permanent state. It's a practice, a return, a gradual easing, like finally exhaling after holding your breath for too long.

Creating a sustainable rhythm meant building breathing room into my life. I learned to recognize when my nervous system needed to reset, when my family needed to slow down, and when saying no actually served our greater well-being. This rhythm honors my need for rest, even when it can't happen every day. Sometimes, it's stolen moments—slowly drinking my morning coffee or standing barefoot on the ground for five minutes while breathing fresh air. Other times, it's bigger choices— choosing something for myself over a household chore or saying no to productivity and yes to simply being.

The key isn't perfect daily rest, but awareness of when I need it and permission to take it when I can. Some days, I slip back into survival mode, and I've learned that's perfectly okay. Some seasons are naturally busier than others. The goal isn't to never struggle; it's to develop awareness and return to a rhythm that serves my life rather than depletes it.

JOY IN UNEXPECTED PLACES

As I built this foundation of presence, regulation, and sustainable rhythm, something unexpected began to emerge. I started to understand joy in a different way. I used to measure joy by the milestones: first steps, words, and major achievements, but this journey asked me to entirely redefine moments of joy and success. Joy began appearing in places others might overlook:

- A fleeting moment of eye contact that feels like a bridge between worlds

- A new sound that represents months or even years of effort

- Spontaneous laughter that bubbles up from nowhere

- A quiet connection between siblings

- A peaceful moment where there used to be overwhelm

- The relief of finally sitting down after a long day

- The sweetness of an unhurried morning

Success in my child started looking like a meltdown that was five minutes shorter than usual, a new food attempted even if not finished, or a moment of peace that once felt impossible. For me, it was also about recognizing my limits before I hit them, asking for help when I needed it, or celebrating small wins instead of rushing to the next goal. I've learned that joy doesn't wait for the perfect moment or a resolved situation. It often meets me right in the middle of the mess: in a chaotic morning that ends with an unexpected shared smile, or laughter that spills out during what should be the hardest hour of the day. Sometimes, joy is found in letting my shoulders drop and my jaw loosen its grip, and just surrendering to not knowing the next move. I've found freedom in releasing control, in laughing through the hard moments, and simply accepting the unexpected instead of trying to manage every outcome.

CHOOSING HOW YOU WANT TO SHOW UP

Out of this foundation of presence and rest, something powerful emerged for me: the ability to choose how I want to show up in my life. It's about pausing long enough to ask myself, *How do I want to be in this moment?* and then making that choice consciously instead of just reacting on autopilot. The questions I ask now are different:

- What do I want our days to feel like, not just look like on paper?

- How can I support my children's growth without making most moments about measurable progress?

- How can I honor both of my children's spirits, celebrating each of their unique needs and abilities?

- What brings genuine peace or connection to our family right now?

- What kind of rhythm honors everyone's needs and my capacity?

- When do I need rest? How can I create space for it?

When I stopped looking outward and started looking inward for guidance, everything shifted. These questions led to meaningful changes in how I lived. I stopped postponing joy until everything was better and started receiving what was already present in my life. I began to understand that taking care of myself wasn't selfish; it was essential to everything else I wanted to create.

STEPPING AWAY WHEN NECESSARY

Part of choosing how to show up meant stepping away from the comparison trap. It meant making choices based on my family's actual needs rather than what I saw while scrolling through social media. The pressure felt relentless. Every day, I was bombarded with curated moments: the perfectly organized sensory bins, the calm therapy sessions, and the milestone celebrations that looked effortless.

Social media has turned parenting into a performance, and special-needs parenting feels especially vulnerable to this pressure. Those curated glimpses aren't real life. They are snapshots of someone's best moments, edited and timed just right. They don't show the meltdowns before the perfect photo, the exhaustion behind the smile, or that the "successful" activity lasted thirty seconds. Taking occasional social media breaks when I needed them helped me step away from external noise and notice my family's authentic moments instead. Once I stopped measuring progress by how much I could fit into my days, I started honoring what felt right for our family's rhythm. I began valuing rest as much as effort, *being* as much as doing, and presence as much as progress.

COMING HOME TO WHAT'S REAL

Presence doesn't erase the hard moments. The challenges don't disappear, the difficult days don't vanish, and the weight of this journey doesn't simply lift. But within the difficulty, I've learned I have choices. I can let pain harden me into bitterness or soften me into the possibility that struggle and beauty can coexist. Often, it just requires extra awareness and patience with myself as I navigate what each moment brings.

Joy is also not a permanent state, but a choice I can return to. A choice to see life in brighter colors despite some hard and consuming moments. I sit with them, feel them, and then make an active choice to release them and welcome joy back in. It's making a courageous choice to not let the hardships of this journey steal you and your child's light. It's nurturing your inner fullness so it can expand and thrive on the outside.

Life still feels overwhelming on many occasions. I slip back into survival mode, into the trap of earning my worth through constant doing. But presence reminds me that even in difficulty, I have the power to find moments of worth in what is rather than waiting for what might be. I'm constantly learning to accept what is. I've practiced forgiving what was. I've made space for rest and release. And somewhere in the middle of it all, something has shifted.

I'm no longer chasing an old version of my life that no longer fits. I'm choosing a new one, rooted in real experience, shaped by hard-won growth, led by love that embraces both struggle and joy. I understand now that rest isn't the opposite of dedication; it's what makes true dedication sustainable. I'm not just surviving this journey anymore. I'm learning to move with it. Shifting between challenge and ease, creating sustainable rhythms, finding beauty in unexpected places. I am present. I am aware. I am becoming who this journey is calling me to be.

READER REFLECTION:
Thriving with Intention

Thriving starts by finding your rhythm and showing up as best you can. The way you move through your days shapes and spills into your family's flow. When you slow down, even just a little, you make room for the good stuff: real connection, fleeting moments of joy, and a pace that feels sustainable.

1. **Recognize your rhythms.** How do I feel when I am running on empty versus when I have my feet on solid ground? What does my body or my mood tell me when I'm rushing around? Are my shoulders tight? Do I have a short fuse? Am I more reactive and scatterbrained?

2. **Find joy in small moments.** What little things light me up when I notice them? How can I make more space to see more wins (mine and my child's)?

3. **Creating sustainable rhythms.** What does thriving look like for us? What works for my energy, my child's needs, and the way we move through life?

4. **Choose "what is" over "what isn't."** Where do I get stuck thinking about what we're missing instead of what's right here? What might shift if I let myself notice what's already enough?

5. **Live with intention.** What's one gentle intention I can hold onto today that will help me feel steadier and more present? What do I want to guide us right now (not as a rule, but as a feeling or a value we're leaning into)?

HEART CONNECTION PRACTICES
(TO DO WITH YOUR CHILD)

- **Daily Joy Practice:** Start or end the day by sharing or writing one small moment of joy. Let it be simple: a laugh, a look, a breath shared. Let it remind you that joy lives in the little things.

- **Symbol Connection:** Choose a meaningful symbol with your child: a heart, star, animal, or a favorite image. Look for it throughout your day together. Let it serve as a quiet reminder of your connection and the calm you can find in each other.

- **Creative Presence:** Dance. Draw. Build. Play. Connect through creativity. This isn't a task-based activity. Shift into the mindset that this creative moment is for the simple joy of being present together.

- **Mirror Moments:** Stand in front of a mirror with your child. Each of you says one kind, true thing about yourself and then one about each other. If your child doesn't use words yet, communicate through their language. Use expressions, gestures, sounds, or movements that feel meaningful to both of you.

AFFIRMATION

I choose to slow down and notice what's already here.
My family is learning to breathe together,
feel together, and find calm together.
Joy lives in the small moments I am present enough to receive.

CHAPTER 12

Becoming

THE INTEGRATION OF IT ALL

For so long, I yearned to reach a different place—one where the weight felt lighter, where I wouldn't feel so lost inside the swirl of appointments, emotions, and uncertainty. I remember wondering, wishing, and hoping for this feeling, but it felt so far away and out of reach. Now, a few years later, I find myself much closer to that feeling that once felt so far away.

Every sleepless night spent researching, every tear, every moment that felt like defeat, and every small victory I celebrated with fierce joy have brought me here. Each challenge was a hidden teacher, shaping my capacity in ways I couldn't yet see. Through this work, this healing, and learning to move through it all, I've rebuilt my foundation. It is now more solid, rooted, and real. The challenges haven't disappeared, and the diagnosis hasn't changed, but the way I face these fears has been transformed, and this is where our power lies: not in controlling the outcome, but in choosing how we meet each moment. I don't always get it right, but I keep showing up and doing my best.

EMBRACING THE FULLNESS OF WHO I AM

Integration isn't about reaching some final, perfect version of yourself. It's a reunion. A weaving together. A remembering of all the parts that brought you here. What I've discovered is that the different versions of ourselves are like messengers, the same way emotions can be. I've learned to think of this process as laying out a welcome mat for different emotions and experiences on this journey. There is room for harder seasons that push us to work through and reflect on our challenges so we can ultimately grow and evolve, but there is also room for lighter moments that make us feel like ourselves because we are more than our pain. Looking back, I can see that I have been many women on this path, each one essential:

- **The new mother, reeling after the diagnosis:** She reminded me that it's okay not to know what comes next, that going into action can be its own form of processing. Feeling the ground shift beneath your feet doesn't mean you're falling; sometimes, it means you're being prepared for new terrain.

- **The tireless researcher:** She showed me the fierce fire of a mother's love. Driven by determination and hope, she proved that love can move mountains when it's paired with action. Her sleepless nights and endless searches mattered; it was love made visible.

- **The woman who raged at broken systems:** She taught me that sacred anger can be fuel for change. Her fury wasn't destructive; it was protective. She refused to accept "that's just how things are" when her child deserved more.

- **The exhausted caregiver:** She revealed that naming your needs is being truthful about your reality. Acknowledging my own humanity wasn't failure; it was necessary for everyone's well-being, including my children's.

- **The grieving dreamer:** She helped me release one vision to make space for another. Through her tears, I learned that letting go of dreams that belong to someone else's story makes room for new dreams that actually fit our family's life.

- **The woman learning to nourish herself:** She showed me that self-care isn't selfish indulgence—it's basic survival. Caring for myself wasn't separate from caring for my family; it was the foundation that made everything else possible.

- **The wife navigating strain and change:** She discovered that relationships can deepen through truth and sustained effort. Love is about daily commitment and conscious choices, especially when it's hard.

Together, these versions form a portrait of resilience, messy truth, and hard-won growth. This shift ultimately allowed me to reclaim the power I once gave to *The Thing*. I no longer live in its shadow. But to understand this, I first had to unravel. I had to learn how to feel without drowning, how to listen to my body, how to calm my nervous system, how to trust myself again. What once felt all-consuming became just one part of my reality, rather than the overwhelming focus.

WHEN HOPE CHANGES SHAPE

As I learned to embrace all parts of my journey, something unexpected happened: My relationship with hope itself began to transform. What has surprised me most is the deep trust I've built in myself and in my daughter's own timing. Early on, hope was tied to outcomes, solutions, and timelines. I was fixated on milestones and markers, needing to see specific progress to believe things were working. Now, hope has become something different. It's about surrender, trusting what comes, and honoring my child's unique way of unfolding. I still hope for progress (that's only human), but it doesn't carry the crushing weight and pressure it once did.

There's a story that holds all of this for me. Each night, for months that stretched into years, I would whisper "*Te amo*" (Spanish for "I love you") to my daughter as I lay with her at bedtime. I didn't know when or if she would be able to say it back. But I whispered it anyway, night after night, like a thread connecting our hearts, holding onto hope without clinging to any specific outcome. I gave those words freely, consistently, and faithfully. And in that offering, I was learning something profound about hope itself. I learned that hope could exist without attachment, and that love given without expectation wasn't wasted, but sacred. Years later, she now says it back every night, adding her own beautiful touch: "*Te amo mucho*" ("I love you a lot").

Hope didn't arrive on my timeline. But it arrived. And it brought with it everything I've learned about trust: Beautiful things can grow slowly, quietly, and often in unseen soil. Love given freely has its own power. Development and connection happen in ways we can't force or predict, but we can create the space for them to unfold naturally. When plans fall apart now, when therapies don't work as expected, and when detours happen, I no longer crumble with them. I pause. I breathe. I ask, "What's next?" I look for where life might be redirecting my family. Each closed door led to deeper wisdom. Each delay taught me patience. Each disappointment revealed new strength I didn't know I had.

HOW THIS JOURNEY TRANSFORMED ME

This journey didn't just change how I parent; it reshaped who I am. The most profound transformation was in how I showed up as a mother to both my children, and how they, in turn, became my greatest teachers (despite giving me some gray hairs along the way).

My daughter, in all her radiance and authenticity, shows me how to delight in the simple and sacred. Her pure joy teaches me to find magic in everyday moments by witnessing her contentment in rediscovering a favorite toy, her excitement in running through the grocery store, announcing her snack to the world, unfazed by others' reactions, and her genuine desire to give hugs and spread love to everyone she meets. She moves through the world with such beautiful authenticity.

My son, with his quiet wisdom and generous spirit, reminds me how compassion can take root even in young hearts. He shows me what quiet strength looks like. It's in the way he patiently sounds out words for his sister, how he naturally adjusts game rules so other children, especially those who struggle, feel included and successful. He has grown into a gentle advocate without even knowing it yet. His zest for life, learning, and fun has also been a powerful reminder for me to let go and live more fully.

Being a mother divided between two children with such different needs has been its own profound teacher. There were seasons when I felt like I was failing them both by giving too much attention to one and not enough to the other. I learned that loving them equally doesn't mean loving them identically. The guilt of divided attention was crushing at times. How can you be fully present for a child melting down while also noticing the other child quietly retreating? How do you celebrate one child's hard-won milestone without overshadowing the other's natural achievements?

I had to learn that being divided doesn't mean being broken. It means expanding. My son taught me that resilience can be quiet, that growth can happen in ways we don't always notice. My daughter taught me that progress isn't linear, that communication comes in many forms, and that joy lives in the smallest victories and in moments that we may overlook. They are my greatest teachers because of how they love. They've taught me that a mother's heart doesn't divide; it multiplies. I've stopped bracing against difficult emotions and started honoring them as messengers. I've released the myth that good parenting means having all the answers. Now, I believe it means being real, being present, and being willing to try again and keep growing.

COMING HOME TO MYSELF

I no longer wait for everything to be figured out before allowing myself to feel peace. I no longer require complete certainty to trust what's unfolding in front of us. Wholeness, I've learned, isn't a destination we finally reach; it's a way of being we choose again and again—with each breath, each reset, and each small act of grace toward ourselves and others. This integration means I can meet difficult moments differently now. When my child has a meltdown, I try to approach it from centeredness rather than panic. When an IEP meeting goes sideways or school plans completely derail, I feel the sting, let it move through me, and then recalibrate from solid ground. When someone says something hurtful or ignorant, I get to choose how I respond. I no longer do so from a place of shame or defensiveness, but from inner power.

Most importantly, I've found my voice. Not just as an advocate for my child, but for myself, too. I can speak up about what I need in relationships, set boundaries that protect my energy, and ask for support without apologizing for being human. I no longer shrink to make others comfortable or accept treatment that doesn't honor my worth or my child's worth. Finding my voice means reclaiming my right to take up space, to have needs, to design a life that fits who I've become rather than following the path that felt most familiar or expected.

TURNING PAIN INTO PURPOSE

This inner transformation created space for something I hadn't anticipated. As I began to heal my heart, a natural desire emerged to extend what I'd learned beyond the walls of my own home. I found community in family, in friends, in professionals who truly saw our family, and in fellow parents walking this road right beside us. Each connection reminded me of a truth I had forgotten: I was never alone. And from that connected place, purpose emerged. Not as some grand mission, but as a quiet call to share what I'd learned through the trenches. The hard-won wisdom I'd gathered through what I have lived so far wasn't meant to stay locked inside my own experience.

Now, I find myself naturally meeting parents wherever they are in their own journeys, sharing resources, insights, and lived experience. When I pass along the name of a therapist who changed everything for my daughter, explain how to navigate confusing government programs, or simply listen as another mother shares her deepest fears, I'm surprised by my own steadiness. Advocacy flows naturally from the solid ground I've found within myself. I finally have the confidence to walk into rooms of professionals, no longer desperate or defensive, open to their guidance, but also trusting my ability to know what my child needs and deserves. Our children deserve environments that honor their unique ways of being, educators who see their unlimited potential rather than their perceived limitations, and communities that genuinely celebrate rather than merely tolerate their differences. This journey gave me wisdom I never asked for, but now that I have it, I know it's meant to be shared so we can all walk forward feeling a little lighter together.

WHERE I STAND NOW

I don't have it all figured out, and I've found peace in that truth. Becoming isn't about reaching some final, complete form. It's about staying open, staying grounded, and finding the courage to keep showing up as ourselves. Uncertainty will always exist. Systems remain inadequate, and every parent (especially a special-needs parent) will always worry. Our children's needs will continue to evolve as they grow, and the unknown will keep stretching ahead. Yet, I've come to recognize this rhythm that plays out across so many seasons of life: disruption, uncertainty, and integration. Now, I meet this progression with a deeper sense of peace and surrender—with more grace for myself and for everyone walking alongside me.

Choosing becoming, day by day, looks like pausing in that space between frustration and reaction. It's how I hold space for my own big emotions without drowning in them. It's the way I listen, *really* listen, when my children speak in their unique languages of need and joy. This journey revealed me to myself. It showed me reserves of love, patience, and resilience I never knew I possessed. But we don't do this inner work just for ourselves. We do it for our families, our communities, for the ripple effects of peace, presence, and awareness we create in every interaction. Mine isn't just a story of survival. It's a story of love, surrender, resilience, and deep transformation. This life may not match the picture I once held in my mind, but it's unapologetically unique and beautiful in ways I'm still discovering.

And if you're still with me, connecting your story to mine in even the smallest way, know this: You are becoming, too, in your own way. Whatever brought you to these words, wherever you are on your journey, trust the process. Trust yourself. Trust that you have everything you need inside you already. We have choices—surviving or thriving, bracing or breathing, hiding or becoming. I can now choose becoming, and for now, that is enough.

READER REFLECTION:
Your Own Becoming

This journey has likely shifted how you see yourself, your child, and perhaps your perspectives on life itself. Take a moment to reflect:

- What aspects of who you are becoming feel most authentic to you now? How has this experience revealed parts of yourself you didn't know existed?

- In what ways do you feel your voice has changed or strengthened through this journey? Has finding your voice been more about personal discovery and empowerment, or do you feel called to share your story more openly?

- How has your sense of purpose evolved? What feels meaningful to you now that might not have before this experience?

- What wisdom or insights from your journey feel important to offer others who might need to hear them?

- As you continue moving forward, what are you most curious about or excited to discover about yourself? What aspects of growth or change do you still feel open to exploring?

AFFIRMATION

I am not who I was, and that's exactly who I am meant to be.
I trust the person I am becoming through this journey.
I am walking forward with my healing heart wide open.

Look How Far We Have Come...

When I first began writing, I didn't set out to create a book. I simply needed space to process everything I was holding—a way to give shape to emotions I had tucked away for so long. Slowly, word by word, it became something else. Something I hoped might hold space for others, too.

Through these pages, I found parts of myself I had forgotten. I also found my voice after years of doubting it even mattered. Sometimes, that meant exposing difficult truths I'd kept hidden, even from myself. Writing this helped me see my own journey: where I started, how far I've come, and where I'm still going. And I hope you've found pieces of yourself here, too.

Through it all, a deeper shift may have started to stir. Not a tidy resolution, but a quiet return to yourself. A growing willingness to see your truth with compassion. A slow turning toward possibility. It didn't happen all at once, and it's not meant to. Every page, every pause, every reflection has been part of something meaningful and brave. Maybe acceptance comes and goes. You don't have to have it all figured out to begin showing up for yourself. Awareness is its own beginning.

I've come to find comfort in the quiet truths I've had to work through on this journey, and continue to work through still. They are the truths that have carried me through the hardest days and continue to guide me: Your emotions are valid, your love is enough, and you and your child are exactly as you're meant to be. You are worthy of care, even in the chaos, and you are never as alone as you may feel.

You are doing important, quiet work (loving, growing, healing) wholeheartedly. So, keep going. Keep noticing the glimmers: the laughter in unexpected places, the softness that sneaks in when you let it. Remember that our healing ripples outward. When we do the work of returning to ourselves, it shows others what is possible. When we find our voice, it creates space for others to find theirs.

As this space continues to evolve, my hope is that it becomes a place where healing can happen in community. Where you can share your voice through your own letters, your reflections, and your story. Your voice and your journey matter.

Thank you for allowing my story to meet yours. That has always been the heart of this offering—not to offer neat answers, but to walk beside you for a moment on a path that can so often feel overwhelming and lonely. Through it all, may you remember that your self-care matters and that your story is still unfolding.

With love and solidarity,

Liz

Writing Forgiveness Letters

As I worked through my own healing, I realized I wasn't just carrying one version of myself—I was carrying many. There was the version of me in the early diagnosis days, raw and terrified. The version navigating the chaos of multiple therapies and specialists. The version who snapped at her partner after another sleepless night. The version who smiled through family gatherings while crumbling inside. Each version of me was frozen in her own moment of pain, and that pain was lingering, spilling into my current life. I needed a way to tell myself, "You did your best. I see you. You are forgiven." So, I wrote to them. One by one.

Writing forgiveness letters to your past selves is about honoring what you went through without carrying the weight of it forward. It's a way of looking back at the versions of yourself who were doing their absolute best in impossible circumstances and offering them the compassion they deserved then and deserve now.

HOW TO WRITE YOUR
FORGIVENESS LETTERS

1. **Identify different versions of yourself.** Think about distinct periods or moments that stand out: a hard moment even before your child was born, receiving confirmation of a *Thing* in your life, a hard season for you or your child (or both), a low relationship point, or a time you felt you failed and didn't feel like you did enough.

2. **Choose one version of yourself to write to.** You can start in chronological order if that feels right, or with the one that feels heaviest right now.

3. **Reflect on what that period felt like.** What did that moment feel like? What were you carrying that no one else could see? What do you feel that you need to tell yourself in that moment? What do you need to let go of and forgive yourself (or someone else) for?

4. **Write the letter:**

    » *"I see you…"* (Acknowledge what you were going through.)

    » *"I forgive you for…"* (Name what you are ready to release.)

    » *"You can lay it down now."* (Give permission to stop carrying it.)

You might write one letter a week for a set period of time, or one comprehensive letter if multiple ones feel overwhelming.

SAMPLE FORGIVENESS LETTER

Dear Hurting Heart,

I see you. Exhausted. Overwhelmed. Trying so hard to hold it all together. I see the long days filled with therapies and worry. I see the nights you lay awake, questioning if you were doing enough. I see the moments when you were too tired to play, too drained to laugh. I see when you felt guilty for it later.

I see the times you felt like you turned away from the people you love most. It wasn't because you didn't care. You were simply drowning and didn't know how to stay afloat.

I forgive you. For the impatience, the tears, the guilt that followed. For the harsh words you said and for the ones you turned inward. For the pressure you put on yourself to do it all. For the moments you felt like you weren't enough when you were giving everything you had. I forgive it all.

You didn't fail. You were doing the best you could in that moment. You showed up even when you had nothing left. You deserved more grace then. You still deserve grace today.

You can lay it all down now. You don't have to carry any of this pain into tomorrow.

With compassion,
Your Healing Heart

After Forgiveness: A Love Letter

Once you've offered forgiveness to your past selves, there's one more letter to write: a love letter to who you are now. This letter isn't about what you survived or what you're sorry for. It's about recognizing the incredible person all those versions of you became. It's about celebrating your strengths, your growth, and the remarkable qualities you've developed. For so long, you have focused on what you did wrong. But what about everything you did *right?* What about the ways you grew? What about the strengths you didn't even know you had? Your love letter might include:

- **Your strengths:** Acknowledge your resilience, your fierce advocacy, and your ability to learn an entirely new language of therapies and diagnoses. Take pride in the way you kept going.

- **Your growth:** Reflect on how you've learned to ask for help, found your voice, stopped apologizing for taking up space, and learned about boundaries.

- **Your qualities:** Notice how your compassion, humor, capacity to love, honesty, and courage have expanded beyond what you thought you were capable of.

- **What you've built:** Recognize the support systems and community you have in your life now. Be proud of the knowledge you've gained that has led to a deeper and more meaningful life.

- **What makes you remarkable:** Give yourself credit for how you have deepened your ability to love with grace and compassion. How you notice when your child is regulated, and how you celebrate their wins. How you hold space for joy. How you've become someone who understands what most people never have to learn.

As you write this letter, don't hold back on praise and the pride you feel in your accomplishments. Step outside of yourself if you have to in order to feel freer in speaking these beautiful truths. Don't forget to add that you are expecting many more wonderful things as time goes on, and that you will have the strength and support to keep on this journey as you always have.

SAMPLE LOVE LETTER

Healing isn't linear. You may write these letters and feel lighter immediately, or you may need to return to them again and again. Be gentle with yourself and your healing heart in progress.

Dear Strong Heart,

Look at you. You made it here. You are still standing, still breathing, still choosing to show up. I want you to know how incredible that is.

You have become so strong. Not the kind that never breaks, but the kind that breaks and still gets back up. You've learned to advocate fiercely, even when your voice shook. You've navigated impossible systems. You've become fluent in a language that was once completely foreign. You've learned to ask for help, and that took more courage than doing it alone ever did.

I love your compassion. Even on the hardest days, you still notice when someone else is struggling. You still show up for your child in ways that matter, even when they're not the ways you imagined.

I love how you've found humor in the chaos: the meltdown in the grocery store, the weird stares when people just don't get it, the endless medical and therapy bills. You've learned to find lightness even when things feel heavy.

You've built something incredible. A network of people who get it. Knowledge that helps not just your family but others walking this road behind you. A home where your child feels safe, seen, and loved exactly as they are.

The small things matter most. The way you celebrate every milestone. The way you notice the sensory preferences, the communication cues, the moments of regulation. The way you've learned that different doesn't mean less.

You are not the parent you thought you'd be. You're better: more real, more resilient, more capable of unconditional love than you ever imagined.

I'm proud of you. Not for being perfect, but for being brave enough to keep growing, keep learning, keep showing up. You are enough. You always have been.

With love and admiration,
Your Becoming Heart

Helpful Resources

These resources offer practical support, emotional grounding, and community connection for families navigating unique needs.

Community & Local Support

- **Parks & Recreation Adaptive Programs:** Many cities offer adaptive sports, sensory-friendly events, inclusive swim lessons, and community activities designed for children with diverse needs. Check your local Parks & Recreation website for current offerings.

- **Parent to Parent USA:** A national network connecting families for peer support, shared experience, and community-based guidance.

- **Family Voices:** A family-led organization offering advocacy, navigation support, and resources for families of children with special health care needs.

- **Parent Training & Information Centers (PTIs):** This is available in every state. PTIs help families understand special education rights, navigate IEPs, and advocate effectively within the school system.

Podcasts for Parenting, Presence, & Self-Care

- **Help Them Bloom—Evelyn Mendal:** Evidence-based conversations on child development, emotional wellness, and conscious parenting.

- **The Special Needs Mom Podcast—Kara Ryska:** Real discussions on identity, burnout, resilience, and the emotional landscape of parenting a child with unique needs.

- **Where They're Planted—Jen Bluske:** Stories and tools for navigating developmental and behavioral challenges.

- **The Mindful Mama Podcast—Hunter Clarke-Fields:** Mindfulness, emotional regulation, and compassionate communication.

- **Good Inside—Dr. Becky Kennedy:** Emotionally informed parenting guidance focused on connection, boundaries, and repair.

- **Beautifully Complex—Penny Williams:** Neurodiversity-affirming support for parents of children with ADHD, autism, or learning differences.

- **Ten Percent Happier—Dan Harris:** Practical meditation tools focused on stress reduction and emotional awareness.

Wellness, Mindfulness, & Emotional Support

- **Kanekshun—Sabrina Badeaux**: Breathwork, Sound Healing, and grounding practices to support emotional regulation and nervous system balance. (Miami based for local clients and offers retreats for group support.)

- **Insight Timer / Calm / Headspace**: Guided meditations, breathing exercises, and relaxation tools for stress and overwhelm.

- **Yoga With Adriene**: Gentle, accessible yoga practices that support grounding, presence, and emotional release.

- **Breathwrk (App)**: Guided breathwork exercises designed to help calm the mind and restore balance.

Mental Health & Psychology

- **Head in the Game—Stephanie Dargoltz, M.S.Ed.**: Compassionate, trauma-informed psychological support for individuals and families navigating emotional or developmental challenges.

- **Hatch + Bloom—Evelyn Mendal, LMHC**: Adult and child support, workshops, and parent-support tools rooted in emotional intelligence, secure attachment, and connection-based parenting.

- **Psychology Today Therapist Finder**: A directory for locating therapists by specialty, approach, insurance, and neurodiversity-informed practice.

Miami Local Support (Optional for South Florida Readers)

- **CARDS—Center for Autism & Related Disabilities:** Free developmental guidance, parent training, school support, and workshops offered throughout Miami-Dade.

- **The Children's Trust (Miami-Dade):** A central hub for family programs, including early childhood services, after-school programs, parent support resources, and inclusive community events.

ABOUT THE AUTHOR

Elizabeth Castillo's journey as a writer began with the search for steadiness as she navigated an unexpected path with her daughter. Without hesitation, she pivoted the trajectory of her life to ensure her daughter had everything she needed. But after years of moving nonstop—physically, mentally, and emotionally—she longed for a way to process, reflect, and reconnect with herself. That longing led to her debut book, *Dear Healing Heart*, where she shares the tender, often unspoken moments of special-needs parenting and the quiet strength that emerges along the way.

A Miami native, Elizabeth lives there with her family, where she continues her own healing journey, learning to savor slower moments of life. Through these intentional steps, she now prioritizes her well-being alongside her family's.

Understanding how lonely and overwhelming special-needs parenting can be, Elizabeth founded Healing Heart Co., where she blends emotional storytelling with supportive products and offerings—reminding parents that their story, healing, and wholeness matter, too.